Bible Supplement

Volumes 5-8

Second Edition

By Jane Claire Lambert & Becky Jane Lambert

Five in a Row Bible Supplement for Volumes 5-8

Second Edition

ISBN 978-1-888659-31-3

Copyright © 1997, 2023 by Jane Claire Lambert and Becky Jane Lambert

Unless otherwise indicated, all scripture quotations are from The ESV® Bible (The Holy Bible, English Standard Version®), copyright © 2001 by Crossway, a publishing ministry of Good News Publishers. Used by permission. All rights reserved.

Published by:
Five in a Row Publishing
312 SW Greenwich Dr.
Suite 220
Lee's Summit, MO 64082
816-866-8500

Send all requests for information to the above address.

All rights reserved. No part of this publication may be reproduced, stored in a retrieval system, or transmitted in any form or by any means—electronic, mechanical, photocopy, recording, or any other—except for brief quotations in printed reviews, without prior permission of the publisher.

Dedicated to our family and friends who continually prayed for us as we wrote these Bible lessons.

Contents

Introduction 7
Bible Verse for Your Geography Lesssons 7

Stories from Volume Five

The Boxcar Children 8
The Raft 16
Snowflake Bentley 18
Betsy Ross: Designer of Our Flag 20
The Gullywasher 31
Minette's Feast 33

Bonus Unit Studies:
Angelo 36
Paper Lanterns 39
The Bravest of Us All 43
The Hatmaker's Sign 47

Stories from Volume Six

Thomas A. Edison: Young Inventor 50
Sarah, Plain and Tall 59
Homer Price 65
The Saturdays 70

Stories from Volume Seven

Helen Keller 75
Skylark 80
The Story of George Washington Carver 87
The Cricket in Times Square 96

Stories from Volume Eight

Neil Armstrong: Young Flyer 104
Marie Curie and the Discovery of Radium 112
Hitty: Her First Hundred Years 119

Helpful Bible Study Materials 130
Afterword 131
Index 132

Five in a Row Bible Supplement

Introduction

We hope that you enjoy the spiritual food you find as you work with this Bible Supplement for the second editions of Volumes 5-8 of *Five in a Row*. But we have just as great a hope that you will mercifully blow away any chaff you discover among the grains. We have prayerfully labored to be helpful, knowing that no work like this will be perfect.

For each *Five in a Row* story to be taught, this Bible Supplement contains an accompanying group of Bible references. We have tried to gather many references so that you might choose one or two that seem the most appropriate to you. As the teacher, you may enjoy reading all the references for a particular story as a Bible study for yourself. Then choose the verse or story that would most enhance the story lesson for your student.

You can teach each Bible concept simply and conversationally. You might say, "Helen doesn't have much self-control right now, does she? The Bible has a few things to say about self-control. Let's take a look at couple of those verses."

Other ways to use this Bible Supplement include memorizing or copying out a verse (for handwriting practice/copywork), adding related worship songs or hymns, or drawing a picture or writing a reflection about the Bible verses you've discussed. You'll find space to record all of these ideas in the Teacher's Notes pages that follow each title.

Carefully consider the age and spiritual readiness of your student to keep the Bible lessons an enjoyable part of your *Five in a Row* study.

Bible Verse for Your Geography Lessons

Consider placing Psalm 113:4 above your map or by your globe when you mention the numerous countries included in *Five in a Row* geography lessons found in Volumes 5-8: "The Lord is high above all nations, and his glory above the heavens!"

The Boxcar Children

Chapter 1—The Four Hungry Children

John 6:35

God has a lot to say about bread in His Word. Henry, Jessie, Violet and Benny were thankful for the bread they bought from the bakery. They cut it into four pieces, ate it and were full. But what about the next morning? Would that one loaf of bread sustain them forever? Of course not. In John 6:35, Jesus tells us He is the **Bread of Life**. Anyone who comes to Him will never go hungry, and he who believes in God will never be thirsty. What does He mean? When we make the decision to ask Jesus into our hearts, we receive an amazing assortment of wonderful gifts! But perhaps the best is the gift of eternal life. Unlike the bread the children bought in the bakery, God's gift of Bread will sustain us for eternity! And all we have to do is ask. We serve a wonderful God!

Chapter 2—Night Is Turned into Day

Genesis 1:1-4

The title of this chapter makes us think of **the first day**. In Genesis 1, God creates the heavens and the earth. In verse 4, we read that God separated the light from the darkness. And He called the light day and the darkness night.

Psalm 118:24

Our Heavenly Father created a wonderful thing for us. He created day, before which there was only a black void. Imagine never seeing anything! Go with your student into a closet, basement or attic without lights or windows. Wait for your eyes to adjust to the darkness. If you've located a truly dark room, you can't see anything. Imagine night never ending! But our Father knows what is best for us. A good verse to remind us to be thankful is found in Psalm 118:24: "This is the day the Lord has made; let us rejoice and be glad in it." Isn't it amazing what the Lord does for us?

Chapter 3—A New Home in the Woods

Psalm 61:4
Psalm 107:29

Henry, Jessie, Violet and Benny find shelter from the storm in a boxcar. They were in a real thunderstorm. Sometimes, life doesn't go quite the way we hope. We get sick right before a special event, our cat runs away, or our dad loses his job. When these things happen, it is like rain on a sunny day. But our Heavenly Father tells us in Psalm 61:4 that we can **take refuge** in the shelter of His wings. In Psalm 107:29, God tells us He can still the storms to a whisper and hush the crashing waves of the sea. He covers us with love and faithfulness and it helps the cloudy times seem less oppressive. The next time something happens that frightens or upsets you, ask God to **quiet your storm**. He will!

Chapter 4—Henry Has Two Surprises

In Proverbs 12:10a, God tells us a wise man cares for his animals. Jessie took good care of Watch. She removed the thorn from his paw, washed the wound, bandaged his paw, held him in her arms and fed him. Sometimes, the way we **care for animals** can be a reflection of how we treat our family and friends. God shares with us in His Word His desire for the treatment of animals. Godly wisdom affects all aspects of our lives—even our relationship with our pets. Learning to be kind to animals and respect them is growing in wisdom.

Proverbs 12:10a

Henry, Jessie, Violet and Benny spend their first night in the boxcar. They are all alone. Does anyone know where they are? God does. In Psalm 139:1-12, God tells us He will always know where we are and **watch over us**. If we go to the jungles of Africa or hide in a closet, He knows. We never need to fear that God has forgotten us or lost us. Our Heavenly Father "hems" us in, according to verse 5, and we cannot be away from Him. Wherever we turn, we find God and His care and protection. What a secure feeling!

Psalm 139:1-12

Chapter 5—The Explorers Find Treasure

The Boxcar children found earthly "treasures." New dishes, a pink cup and wheels are certainly fun, but they won't last forever. The Bible teaches about storing up **treasures in heaven**. In Luke 12:22-24, Jesus talks about a treasure that will never go away!

Luke 12:22-24

If you buy a new bicycle, no matter how many locks you put on it or where you store it, a thief might be able to steal it from you. And in any event, it will eventually grow old and rusty. But when we have the love of God in our hearts, no one can take it away. It is an eternal treasure of great worth! The love of God is a treasure that anyone can have. Poor or rich, old or young, prosperous or struggling—all people can receive the most important gift of all.

Five in a Row Bible Supplement

Proverbs 8:19-21 — In Proverbs 8:19-21, the Lord tells us His gifts are better than gold or silver! He bestows heavenly wealth on us and He makes our treasuries full. Next time you want to buy something and don't have quite enough money, think of all the heavenly gold you have and be happy! Allowances and earned money may come and go, but your treasures from God are here to stay.

Chapter 6—A Queer Noise in the Night

Henry and Jessie are frightened by the noise in the woods. Talk with your student about times he has been frightened. Share with your student times you have been frightened.

Psalm 23

Psalm 91:5
Psalm 27:1
Isaiah 41:10

Perhaps the most significant aspect of **fear** is thinking we are alone. But we are not alone! In His Word in Psalm 23, Jesus tells us we do not have to fear. Even if we walk through a dark valley, He is there. Read this beautiful and calming psalm together. Psalms 91:5 and 27:1 and Isaiah 41:10 are verses about God's omnipresence and how we need not fear. Next time you are frightened remember God is near and be of strong faith!

Chapter 7—A Big Meal From Little Onions

Henry asks Jessie if it would be appropriate to build a swimming pool on Sunday. Why? Henry knows that Sunday is considered a day of rest. The Bible tells us God created the world in six days and then rested on the seventh day (Genesis 2:2). This seventh day is considered the Christian's **day of rest** as well. It is called the Sabbath.

Genesis 2:2

Exodus 20:8
Deuteronomy 5:12

Exodus 20:8 and Deuteronomy 5:12 both admonish us to observe the Sabbath. Instead of working and tending to our own busy lives, the Sabbath is our opportunity to reflect on our week, honor God, attend church and quiet ourselves for the week to come. Just as our bodies need rest to rejuvenate, so do our spirits. Next Sunday, think of Henry asking his question and take some time to relax and thank God for His blessings!

Chapter 8—A Swimming Pool at Last

Henry measured the depth of the brook with a stick. When we **measure** something, we know exactly what size it is. Henry knew the brook was 12 inches deep by looking at the watermark left on the stick. But some things cannot be measured. No matter how hard we try, there are some things which cannot be defined by size.

In Ephesians 3:17-19, the apostle Paul writes a prayer for the Ephesians. His prayer for them is that they might begin to understand the width, length, height and depth of God's love.

Ephesians 3:17-19

How do you measure love? It is impossible. God loves us so much we cannot comprehend it. His love is able to do more for us than we can even ask. Paul says God's love surpasses the knowledge of man. Imagine—God's love for His children is infinite! It is without beginning or end, has no limits and isn't determined by our actions. Study these verses about our Father's heart—John 3:16, 1 John 4:19, 2 Thessalonians 3:5—and rest in the knowledge of God's amazing love for you!

John 3:16
1 John 4:19
2 Thessalonians 3:5

Chapter 9—Fun in the Cherry Orchard

Mrs. Moore, the doctor's mother, graciously tells the children to eat "all you want" of the cherries. But the book tells us Henry and the other children do not eat all they want, but instead only occasionally pop a ripe cherry into their mouths.

Greed is an ugly human characteristic. Being greedy means we take all we can get, not thinking of others and their needs. If there are two pieces of cake left on the plate, a greedy person would grab the largest piece first. A gracious person would offer the larger piece to the other person.

The Bible talks about avoiding greed in Luke 12:15. Jesus tells us to be on guard against all types of greed. He says a person's life is much more than a bunch of material possessions, food or drink. Being gracious instead of being greedy is

Luke 12:15

Five in a Row Bible Supplement

the godly way to live our lives. It makes others glad to be around us, makes us happier, and pleases the heart of our Father. Other verses dealing with greed are Proverbs 15:27, 1 Peter 5:2 and Romans 1:29. Let your heart trust God to supply your needs and be gracious to others!

Chapter 10—Henry and the Free-for-All

Henry ran a terrific race! Long, steady strides and concentration helped him win the prize. In the Bible, God tells us that our lives as Christians are very much like a foot race. We must keep our eyes focused on the prize and **run with perseverance** (Philippians 3:13-14, Hebrews 12:1). At first, Henry felt like running just for fun. But as he continued, he realized he had a realistic chance of winning the silver cup.

We know we will win our prize (eternal life with Christ) if we continue to glorify God, obey Him, love others and stay true to our beliefs. Sometimes, however, it gets difficult. Someone makes us angry, we see bad things happening to good people (wars, famines, floods, shootings, etc.) on the news and in our neighborhoods, or our siblings fight with us. The Word of God tells us to keep the faith (2 Timothy 4:7) and run as if we planned on getting the prize (1 Corinthians 9:24). God will help us all along the way and we can be excited at the prospect of seeing Him waiting for us at the finish line!

Chapter 11—The Doctor Takes a Hand

Benny knew Dr. Moore would not leave Violet—even for $5,000. Benny knew the doctor understood that people are more important than money. The Bible tells us to respect and love our neighbor as much as we love ourselves (Leviticus 19:18). This means that when we think of saying or doing something to someone, we should stop and think how we would feel if it were said or done to us. Sometimes this is easier said than done!

In the book of Matthew, some priests asked Jesus what was **the greatest commandment** of all (Matthew 22:36-40). Jesus said loving the Lord with all our being is the greatest commandment. Then He said the second greatest commandment is to love our neighbor as we love ourselves.

People are more important than any material possession we could ever have, because people are created in God's image. Even when we know what we are supposed to do, how do we learn how to love people? First Corinthians 13 tells us that love is patient, kind, not envious, humble, gracious, and keeps no record of wrongs. Here are some additional verses about loving people and putting them above material things: James 2:8, 1 Peter 1:22 and 3:8, 1 John 3:10 and 4:21. Dr. Moore had his priorities straight. May we also have such love for our friends and our Savior!

1 Corinthians 13

James 2:8
1 Peter 1:22
1 Peter 3:8
1 John 3:10
1 John 4:21

Chapter 12—James Henry and Henry James

The children did not **recognize** their grandfather at first. Henry did not know Mr. Alden was the man who gave him the prize on Field Day. It wasn't until Henry had spent some time with him and listened to him talk that Henry finally realized who Mr. Alden was.

A similar incident occurs in Luke 24:13-35. The disciples are walking along, discouraged and frightened after Jesus has been crucified. Suddenly Jesus appears to them and begins walking with them. Read the humorous conversation as the disciples attempt to explain to Jesus all the recent events about His own death! Finally, after spending time together and having dinner, the disciples recognize Jesus for the first time (verse 31).

Luke 24:13-35

Luke 24:31

One of the most important ways we can come to "recognize" Jesus is by listening to His "voice" and His words. By reading His Word and developing a regular prayer life we eventually learn to recognize the voice of Jesus when He is speaking to our hearts. Consider developing a plan for at least a few minutes of Bible reading daily with your student, and encourage him to set aside at least a short time each day to pray.

Chapter 13—A New Home for the Boxcar

The boxcar children are happy at last! At home with their grandfather and Watch, they know many happy times are ahead. As children of God, we too can rest in the knowledge of happy times. Our Father delights in giving **good gifts**

2 Corinthians 9:15	to His children (2 Corinthians 9:15). Henry and the children were afraid that Watch would be taken away from them. They needed to trust God to provide them with all good things.
Psalm 26:1 Psalm 56:4 Proverbs 3:5 Proverbs 28:26 Isaiah 25:9 Romans 8:28	We can trust the Lord to supply all our needs and we have no need to fear. The following verses talk about the importance of **trusting** our Heavenly Father: Psalms 26:1 and 56:4, Proverbs 3:5 and 28:26, and Isaiah 25:9. Think about how all things work together for good (Romans 8:28) for followers of Christ!

Teacher's Notes

The *Teacher's Notes* are optional but provide a space for you to document which Bible verse you choose and any other discussion points, songs, verses or notes you wish to keep record of for your student.

THE BOXCAR CHILDREN

Date:

Student:

Five in a Row **Bible Verse(s):**

☐ Memorized Verse(s) / Copywork

Character Trait or Life Lesson to apply:

Related Worship Songs/Hymns

Misc. Notes:

Have your student draw a picture or write a reflection on the Bible verse(s) in the space below.

Five in a Row Bible Supplement

The Raft

Romans 8:28 — Romans 8:28 says that **all things work together for good**. If Nicky had this verse committed to memory, he might have used it to gain strength as he watched his father's car pull away from Grandma's and felt the disappointment of separation, and the eeriness of a summer spent in unfamiliar territory.

How might this verse have helped Nicky? Can your student think of times when this verse could be of help to him?

John 21:2-8 — The part of the story where Grandma tells Nicky where to fish reminds us of a story in John 21:2-8. The disciples had been out all night fishing and had come back in the morning with empty boats. They meet Jesus on the shore and he tells them to go back out and cast their nets on the other side of the boat. Now, the disciples could have done what Nicky did. They could have looked around and decided they knew better than Jesus where to cast. But they didn't. The disciples (even though they were not sure it would work) cast their nets where Jesus indicated and they pulled in so many fish their boats were almost sinking! Does your student think that Nicky probably would have caught some fish if he had been teachable and fished for the bluegill where Grandma said? (At least he would have had a better chance.)

You could tie in the chapters about Noah to *The Raft* by discussing the raft and all the **animals** that Nicky sees that summer. Nicky's raft is a type of boat and has the animals drawn all over it and some even sitting on it, reminding us of a boat long ago that housed and saved all the animals of the earth! (Genesis 6:14-22)

Genesis 6:14-22

Hebrews 13:5b — If Nicky felt at first like he had been sort of **left behind** by his father, he might have remembered his Heavenly Father who it says in Hebrews 13:5b, I will never leave you or forsake you. That is God's Word, and Nicky would have been able to count on that no matter how he felt.

Teacher's Notes

The *Teacher's Notes* are optional but provide a space for you to document which Bible verse you choose and any other discussion points, songs, verses or notes you wish to keep record of for your student.

THE RAFT

Date:

Student:

Five in a Row **Bible Verse(s):**

☐ Memorized Verse(s) / Copywork

Character Trait or Life Lesson to apply:

Related Worship Songs/Hymns

Misc. Notes:

Have your student draw a picture or write a reflection on the Bible verse(s) in the space below.

Five in a Row Bible Supplement

Snowflake Bentley

Isaiah 1:18
Psalm 51:7

Matthew 28:3

When reading *Snowflake Bentley* with your student, you may wish to remind him of verses in the Bible that have **snow** in their wording. Isaiah 1:18 speaks of "sins becoming white as snow" through the work of the Lord. In Psalm 51:7, a repentant sinner's prayer, the petitioner asks for the Lord to purify him and wash him so he will be "whiter than snow". When Jesus rose from the dead, Matthew 28:3 says that he had the appearance of lightning and his raiment was white as snow.

Genesis 8:22
Matthew 24:12
John 18:18

Remind your student that the Vermont winters where Wilson Bentley lived are quite cold. There are some interesting Bible verses that are connected with the idea of **cold**. Genesis 8:22 speaks of heat and cold tied in to a promise! In Matthew 24:12 Jesus warns of people's love growing cold, and in the story of Peter's denial of Jesus it says in John 18:18 that he was warming himself at a fire because it was cold.

Psalm 8

Wilson Bentley was captivated by the **beauty** he saw in the **natural world** around him. He reminds us of the many psalms that joyously speak of the wonders the Lord has created. Read some of these with your student as you marvel, along with the psalmist and Bentley, over the beauties in nature. (Psalm 8)

Not only did Snowflake Bentley see marvels in nature and enjoy them for himself, he was **passionate** in his desire to share and make known the beauty he saw around him. This reminds us of sharing the good news of Jesus Christ. For those who have experienced the wonders of forgiveness and the beauty of the Lord's holiness, the marvel of the Holy Spirit filling and guiding causes a passionate desire to share, to show, to find some way to help others to meet the Lord for themselves!

Teacher's Notes

The *Teacher's Notes* are optional but provide a space for you to document which Bible verse you choose and any other discussion points, songs, verses or notes you wish to keep record of for your student.

SNOWFLAKE BENTLEY

Date:

Student:

Five in a Row **Bible Verse(s):**

☐ Memorized Verse(s) / Copywork

Character Trait or Life Lesson to apply:

Related Worship Songs/Hymns

Misc. Notes:

Have your student draw a picture or write a reflection on the Bible verse(s) in the space below.

Five in a Row Bible Supplement

Betsy Ross: Designer of Our Flag

Chapter 1—The Choice

Betsy feels that no one understands her! She is a girl but she likes wood and building things. Betsy is an individual and God created her that way. Her brother George tries to "pigeon-hole" Betsy with all little girls, but she is her own, unique person. Does your student ever feel **misunderstood**? We have all felt like that many times. When we begin to believe no one understands us, a little root of bitterness creeps into our hearts. Soon we aren't being as kind as we should be. What we must always remember is that all people (our mother and father, siblings, strangers and friends) will misunderstand us sometimes, but there is One who never will!

Psalm 56:8

In Psalm 56:8 David is speaking to God and acknowledging that God knows and remembers all of his pains and sorrows. He knows every time we feel misunderstood and sad!

The next time your student is feeling confused or betrayed, remind him that his Heavenly Father is thinking of him and loving him. Nothing escapes the love of our Father!

Chapter 2—The Sour Dough

Betsy and her mother work hard at making delicious bread for their family. Bread is sometimes called the "staff of life" because of how integral it is to the world's diet. As believers in Jesus, we are invited to share in a sacred ceremony which includes bread. Sometimes called Communion, the Sacrament or the **Lord's Supper,** the Bible teaches us to set aside a special time to partake of this Communion meal, in remembrance of Jesus.

Luke 22:19

Jesus Himself was the first to lead people in this special meal. The story of that event is found in Luke 22:19. Jesus, at what we now call the Last Supper, sat around a table with His twelve disciples. He drank a sip from the cup and gave instruction that we were to do the same in remembrance of His blood, shed for our sins. Then He broke off a piece of bread and ate it, instructing us to eat the bread in remembrance of His body, broken for us.

Communion is a time for us to reflect on our thankfulness for Jesus, His sacrifice for us and the goodness of God in our lives, as well as the hope of His return. It is both somber and joyful!

Chapter 3—Peppermint Stick Candy

George's nose is pressed against the windowpane. He can't wait until Betsy comes home at the end of the day so he won't be alone and he can play with her. In the Bible, the Lord tells us to be ever **watchful** for His return to us! In Psalm 130:6, the psalmist says that his soul watches for the Lord intensely. In fact, he says that he watches more intently than the night watchman watches for morning. When you think about the Lord and you watch for Him, remember the picture of George waiting for Betsy's return—his nose pressed against the windowpane.

Psalm 130:6

Chapter 4—The Wagon Ride

Debby and Edwin are husband and wife now! This is a special time for the Griscomb family, because Debby is their first child to be married. Does your student know there are wonderful accounts of **marriage** in the Bible?

Sit down and share with your student the beautiful tale of Rebekah and Isaac (Genesis 24). Their meeting and marriage was certainly unusual, yet God-ordained and miraculous!

Genesis 24

Abraham, Isaac's father, sends out his servant to find a suitable mate for his son. The servant prays to God and asks Him for a sign—something to signify to him that he has indeed found the right woman. A short while later, he finds Rebekah, and after approaching her father, he asks her if she would be willing to accompany him back to Abraham's camp to marry Isaac! Imagine—Rebekah has never met or even seen Isaac. She will have to leave her family and travel, in order to marry him! But Rebekah obeys God and goes to Isaac. In the final verse of this chapter, the Bible says that Isaac married Rebekah and he loved her.

(You may want to tell a simplified story of the marriage of Ruth and Boaz, as another example.)

Ruth

Five in a Row Bible Supplement

Chapter 5—The Visit

Benjamin Franklin's witty sayings have been popular for well over 200 years! His "kernels" of wisdom are easy to remember and each one shares a simple truth. Does your student know the Bible has a **book of sayings** very similar to Mr. Franklin's? It's called the Book of Proverbs.

Proverbs 3:1
Proverbs 3:28
Proverbs 10:12
Proverbs 10:19
Proverbs 10:27
Proverbs 13:12
Proverbs 17:22

Written by the wisest man to ever live, King Solomon, Proverbs is filled with small sayings, sometimes called "maxims." A maxim is a true statement, described in a minimum of words and in a memorable way. Share with your student some of the most famous (or your favorite!) proverbs (3:1, 3:28, 10:12, 10:19, 10:27, 13:12, 17:22).

The Lord's wisdom can have very practical applications in our daily life. Perhaps your student would like to select a proverb each week for his family to read and share. He might even want to create a little booklet of his favorite proverbs. Perhaps your whole family can memorize the verse.

Proverbs 3:1-2

Enjoy reading the wise words of King Solomon with your student. Remind him to keep the Lord's wisdom close to his heart because it will give him life (Proverbs 3:1-2)!

Chapter 6—The New School

Betsy is glad to be herself. So is Susannah! We are all **different and special** in our own way. What does your student think makes him special? What are his strengths? His weaknesses? Does your student know that no two people's fingerprints are alike? Isn't that amazing? No two people are alike, but our Heavenly Father knows each of us perfectly because He created us—He actually made us within our mothers' wombs.

Psalm 139

Share with your student the amazing 139th Psalm. Filled with the testimony of God's love for us and His encompassing knowledge about us, this psalm is both awesome and comforting.

The Lord knows when we get up in the morning and when we go to bed at night. He knows what we're thinking all the time and he even knows what we are going to say, before we say it! Surely a Father who is this concerned with His children is a Father worth trusting!

Chapter 7—Something Exciting

"The wind was rising higher every minute. Dark clouds raced across the sky... The big ship rolled from side to side." Betsy loves the exciting **storm** because she is safely on shore and in no real danger. Does your student know a story from the Bible about another ship in a storm? It is found in Mark 4:35-41 and in Matthew 8:23-27. We read that Jesus is out in a boat with His disciples. Soon, Jesus falls asleep. Suddenly, a storm begins. Unlike Betsy, the disciples are frightened and believe the boat is going to sink! They wake Jesus up. They are terrified by the powerful storm. Jesus, filled with the power of God, simply rebukes the wind and rain, and the sea is instantly calm.

Mark 4:35-41
Matthew 8:23-27

Jesus has authority, even over the weather! We must never forget our Savior's power, even as we remember His gentleness.

Chapter 8—The Sovereign

In our story, Betsy receives a beautiful gold coin! The Bible talks about **coins** as well. There are many stories you may share with your student, but here are a couple of the most familiar.

In Luke 15:8-10, Jesus tells one of His parables (or stories). In this parable, a woman has ten silver coins, but loses one. When she discovers it's missing, she cleans the house from top to bottom until she finds it. After the lost coin is found, she calls all of her friends and has a huge party to celebrate the discovery! Jesus likens this persistent search and celebration to the way Heaven rejoices when someone accepts Christ as their Savior and becomes a Christian. For every sinner who is saved, much joy is shared among the angels!

Luke 15:8-10

Luke 21:1-4 Another famous story in the Bible involving coins is found in Luke 21:1-4. In this tale, Jesus remarks on seeing people giving their offerings at the temple one day. He tells the disciples that all of the rich people contribute huge amounts of money to the temple treasury. But one woman, a poor widow, placed two small coins into the treasury. Those two coins were all she had in the world. Jesus said her offering was of more importance than all the others, because she had sacrificed everything she owned, while the others had given merely a small portion of their wealth.

In both stories, the coins seem to symbolize our hearts, not our actual money. May we all be willing to give the Lord all we have in our hearts!

Chapter 9—Ice Skates in July

Betsy has hoped for a pair of skates for a very long time. Finally, she has the money to buy them. But it's July! She has to wait many months for winter to come, so she can use them.

Proverbs 13:12 In Proverbs 13:12, the Bible tells us that when **hope** is deferred (unfulfilled for a long time) the heart can grow sick. In other words, when we hope for something and it begins to seem like it will never happen, sometimes we can get discouraged and sad. What are some things you've hoped for and never received?

But there is a second part to Proverbs 13:12 that is very exciting! The second line of that verse says that a hope fulfilled (when it finally happens) is a tree of life. When we hope for something and it doesn't seem to be happening, we can grow weary. We tire of persistently unmet expectations and unfulfilled dreams. However, there will come a time when our hopes will be answered and that is like a tree of life!

The next time your student grows weary or sad, remind him of this verse—the second part—and pray that hope will again fill his heart!

Chapter 10—Philadelphia Winter

Betsy and George are sent to fetch the doctor for their ill father. Doctors are gifted and highly trained individuals who are able to do many healing things for our bodies. But no person can **heal** us as quickly and miraculously as our Heavenly Father.

In Exodus 15:26, the Lord tells us that He is the one who heals us! In the Bible, Jesus was often called upon to heal the sick. Share with your student the many stories of Jesus' healing power. In Matthew 9:1-8, Jesus heals a paralytic. In Matthew 9:27-31, Jesus heals the blind and mute. In Mark 10:46-52, Jesus heals blind Bartimaeus.

Exodus 15:26

Matthew 9:1-8
Matthew 9:27-31
Mark 10:46-52

In Matthew 9:35, the Bible tells us Jesus walked through the towns and villages, preaching the blessed news of salvation and healing every illness and disease. Jesus brought both healing of the soul and healing of the body. When we are sick, our Heavenly Father can still heal us. Sometimes He heals us directly. At other times, He heals us through physicians such as the doctor who cared for Betsy's father. Our God is a sovereign God who responds to our faith and acts in His mercy!

Matthew 9:35

Chapter 11—The Contest

Mr. Griscomb tells his children about the importance of keeping the Word of God always before their eyes. He exhorts them to remember the wisdom of the Bible and to follow its ways. Mr. Griscomb has the right idea!

The Bible uses a special word to describe the way we should dwell on the Word of God: **meditate**. To meditate means to think continuously about something and to reflect on it at all times. This is the way God wants us to study His Word.

Show your student the following verses in Psalms: 119:15, 119:78 and 119:97. In Proverbs 2:1-5, the Bible tells us that if we store up the commands of the Lord in our heart and search for understanding, then we will be granted the fear of the Lord. Encourage your student to keep the Word of God before him and to hide it in his heart!

Psalm 119:15
Psalm 119:78
Psalm 119:97
Proverbs 2:1-5

Five in a Row Bible Supplement

Chapter 12—The Quotation

In our lessons for this chapter, we learned about the structure and history of the **Bible**. For those of us who know God and obey his commands, the Bible is much more than just a popular group of sayings and stories. We believe it is inspired and provides us with a "road map" of directions for living a pleasing life. The Scriptures include both comforting words of love from our Heavenly Father to us, and warnings from Him for our daily living—ways to avoid pitfalls and disappointment.

1 Peter 1:25

In 1 Peter 1:25, the Bible tells us that the Word of God will endure forever! It is a living testament to God's power and goodness. Studying the Bible is a wonderful way to learn about the history of our faith and to learn to appreciate the beautiful writings. But never forget—the Bible is not a compilation of sweet stories, but the sacred expression of God's own Word. What a wonderful thing to have! Treasure it and keep it close to your heart always.

Chapter 13—The Sampler

Matthew 2:1-12

Betsy spends a long time sewing the beautiful five-pointed stars on her sampler. **Stars** play an important part in the Bible. Does your student remember the tale of the wise men (Matthew 2:1-12)? The wise men followed the bright, shining evening star in the east to the place where Jesus was living with Mary and Joseph.

What do you think that special star looked like? It must have been especially bright, to catch the eyes of the wise men. Imagine them seeing that twinkling, celestial body and walking under its light all the way to Bethlehem.

Jesus is sometimes called our Morning Star (Venus, known as the morning star, is a very bright light in the sky that appears just before dawn). In addition, when we see the sun ("son") or feel its warmth, we can reflect on the light God shines on us each day. And when we act in a godly manner, we are able to reflect that warmth back to others. What a special shining cycle!

Chapter 14—Booths for the Fair

Hannah loves her sister Betsy and believes in her ability and workmanship. Are believing in someone and loving them the same thing? Not really, but the two often go hand in hand. The Bible speaks about **love** in hundreds of verses, but there is one special chapter in 1 Corinthians which talks about love more than any other—the thirteenth chapter. Share with your student this beautiful passage. Draw his attention to the seventh verse in this chapter.

1 Corinthians 13

1 Corinthians 13:7

Among other things, God defines love as protecting, believing and hoping. Loving someone means we believe in who they are, including their gifts and abilities. And those we believe in, we most often love. And it is the same for God. He loves and believes in us and that is a comforting thought!

Chapter 15—Today and Tomorrow

When Betsy arrives at the booth at five o'clock, the crowd is so large she can't see the platform! George, her little brother, is very short but keeps jumping up and down trying to see what is happening.

There is a similar story in the Bible in Luke 19:1-10. Jesus came to a city called Jericho to preach the gospel. The crowds swarmed around Jesus as he walked through the town. A certain man, named **Zacchaeus**, was too short to see Jesus. He tried but, frustrated, he finally gave up and ran ahead of the crowd. Climbing a sycamore tree, Zacchaeus sat in the branches high above the people where he was able to catch a glimpse of Jesus.

Luke 19:1-10

When Jesus reached the spot where Zacchaeus was perched, He slowed down and looked up into the tree. The crowd must have stopped, too, and everyone looked up at Zacchaeus. Jesus called out to him, and told him to come down from the tree. Zacchaeus climbed down out of the tree and was welcomed gladly by Jesus.

Five in a Row Bible Supplement

The story of Zacchaeus is a wonderful tale of redemption. He was a dishonest tax collector, but his brief encounter with Jesus changed his life forever. Immediately, he began to repay the people he had cheated and began to follow Jesus!

Share this story with your student and remind him—it is never too late to be greeted by the Master.

Chapter 16—The Apprentices

The Colonists are divided in their allegiance to their homeland. They do not think the authority of England should be placed on them any longer. The question of **authority and allegiance** is found in the Bible, too.

Matthew 22:15-22

In Matthew 22:15-22, the Bible suggests where we should place our devotion. Caesar, the ruler of the land in Jesus' day, demanded taxes. Jesus tells the people to pay Caesar whatever taxes they owe, but to give to God what belongs to Him. What does He mean?

Jesus is saying that although there are earthly rulers and authorities, they are placed in those positions by God. He is over all things. We must honor and respect our earthly authorities, but we must never forget that we owe God our full allegiance. Only He deserves our worship!

Chapter 17—A Famous Story

Sadly, Betsy Ross was left a widow at a very early age. Her husband John was killed in an explosion. Betsy was forced to continue the family upholstery business alone. She remarried later, but for several years Betsy was on her own.

James 1:27
Deuteronomy 10:18

The Bible has many things to say about **widows**. Challenging believers to serve and care for them with compassion is the central theme of both James 1:27 and Deuteronomy 10:18. God, in His infinite love, knows the pain of loneliness and seeks to comfort all those who are oppressed.

As His "hands and feet" on Earth, we can share in this special service by loving, caring and serving those who are weak. Not only the widow, but the orphan, the immigrant, the homeless, the sick and the dying. Acting in this manner, we not only make our Heavenly Father's heart happy, but we become more noble human beings. Isn't it wonderful that we are allowed to help the Lord with His work? Isn't it glorious He is willing to use us?

Teacher's Notes

The *Teacher's Notes* are optional but provide a space for you to document which Bible verse you choose and any other discussion points, songs, verses or notes you wish to keep record of for your student.

BETSY ROSS: DESIGNER OF OUR FLAG

Date:

Student:

Five in a Row Bible Verse(s):

_____
_____
_____
_____
_____
_____
_____
_____

☐ Memorized Verse(s) / Copywork

Character Trait or Life Lesson to apply:

_____
_____

Related Worship Songs/Hymns

_____
_____
_____
_____
_____

Misc. Notes:

_____
_____
_____
_____
_____
_____
_____
_____

Have your student draw a picture or write a reflection on the Bible verse(s) in the space below.

The Gullywasher

Open *The Gullywasher* to the beautiful picture of grandfather asleep on the ground. The graceful hummingbird is taking strands of his dark hair. Remind your student of the amazing fact that the Lord knows **every hair** on your student's head! According to Matthew 10:30, the Lord even has them numbered.

Matthew 10:30

The Gullywasher is by definition of title about a **great storm**. Leticia and her Abuelito watch a real gullywasher at the beginning of the story and then grandfather tells her a tall storm tale about the "big one." He says that the rain from the storm had wrinkled his hands. This might be a good time to read some verses about the really big rain—the Flood from Genesis. Or you could talk about Jesus actually calming a storm, Luke 8:22-25, or of Paul and the men he was with during storm and their shipwreck: Acts 27:14-44.

Genesis 7
Luke 8:22-25
Acts 27:14-44

There are also many references to **rain** in the Bible. There are verses about times of no rain, and verses about time of spring and latter rains. Elijah dealt with a period of drought: James 5:17-18. You could tie any of these references or incidents to *The Gullywasher* and have a great conversation about God and His Word.

James 5:17-18

After telling of the worst storm he ever saw, Leticia's grandfather says that he saw the **reflection** of his face in the water. James 1:23-24 is a verse that makes the comparison of us looking at our reflection in a mirror then going away and forgetting what we looked like, to people who look in God's Word who understand what they are to do and then go away and forget to do it. The story tie-in here is loose; it is simply based on the word "reflection" to remind us of that reference in the Bible.

James 1:23-24

Once again the incredible beauty of God's creation shines through the illustrations in *The Gullywasher*. Look for a while at the page with the large bird called the roadrunner and the small view of the grandfather sleeping. There is so much beauty in the flowers, trees, and the many animals, as well as the sky and the clouds. After looking at all the lovely landscape, read some psalms that praise God for his magnificent creation. Try singing (creating a tune) some of these psalms. Or try along with your student psalm-like praise yourself.

Five in a Row Bible Supplement

Teacher's Notes

The *Teacher's Notes* are optional but provide a space for you to document which Bible verse you choose and any other discussion points, songs, verses or notes you wish to keep record of for your student.

THE GULLYWASHER

Date:

Student:

Five in a Row **Bible Verse(s):**

☐ Memorized Verse(s) / Copywork

Character Trait or Life Lesson to apply:

Related Worship Songs/Hymns

Misc. Notes:

Have your student draw a picture or write a reflection on the Bible verse(s) in the space below.

32 *The Gullywasher*

Minette's Feast

The Lord designed us to be relational and enjoy fellowship with Him and with other people. Many times in the Bible He uses **meals** as a way for His followers to share their lives and their faith while doing something as simple as eating. We have to eat to survive, but God desires so much more than just survival for us. He wants us to thrive physically, spiritually and in our relationships.

Our meals with our family and with others are not just about the food. They are about fellowship: sharing our lives with each other, reconnecting after time away from each other (at work or school) and celebrating our relationships!

The Last Supper (Matthew 26:26-29) is a well known example of Jesus using everyday food and drink to connect with His disciples and give them, and us, a tool to remember Him daily.

Matthew 26:26-29

Another less common verse that demonstrates God's plan for meals to be a time of fellowship is found in Acts 2:42 and 46. In these verses, we see the early believers not only breaking bread (eating) together but also doing so with glad and sincere hearts and prayers. This is what we do when we pray and eat together as a family or with friends. We create an environment that allows for fellowship and relationships, as well as our physical bodies, to be fed.

Acts 2:42 & 46

Julia, encircled by the delicious scent wafting off of the roast, is graciously bringing it to the table for dinner with friends. She didn't make the magnificent roast (that took days for the flavor to develop) for herself or even for herself and Paul. No, she made it for a special time of fellowship with others. This is a beautifully illustrated example of breaking bread together with glad and sincere hearts!

Juila is determined to improve her cooking. Discuss with your student what Julia does to get better at cooking. On the page with Julia and Chef Bugnard at Le Cordon Bleu and the page opposite of that, the text tells us that Julia **sought advice** from people at the market and learned from cookbooks. Finally she signed up to take classes at a cooking school—a place she could learn from a teacher.

Five in a Row Bible Supplement   33

Ask your student what areas he is working to improve in his life and what he's doing to get better at those things.

For example, we listen to our teachers and do schoolwork to gain knowledge. We listen to our bosses to get better at our jobs. The Bible is the place for believers to go to seek advice and learn from the ultimate teacher: Jesus. For example …

Matthew 6:9-13   Jesus shows us how to pray in Matthew 6:9-13:

"Pray then like this: Our Father in heaven, hallowed be your name, your kingdom come, your will be done, on earth as it is in heaven. Give us today our daily bread. And forgive us our debts, as we also have forgiven our debtors. And lead us not into temptation, but deliver us from evil."

John 3:16   In John 3:16 He teaches us how to be saved:

"For God so loved the world that he gave his only Son, that whoever believes in him shall not perish but have eternal life."

It's not just children that need to learn or get better at things. Julia shows us that adults also need to be humble and learn from others to gain knowledge!

Teacher's Notes

The *Teacher's Notes* are optional but provide a space for you to document which Bible verse you choose and any other discussion points, songs, verses or notes you wish to keep record of for your student.

MINETTE'S FEAST

Date:

Student:

Five in a Row **Bible Verse(s):**

☐ Memorized Verse(s) / Copywork

Character Trait or Life Lesson to apply:

Related Worship Songs/Hymns

Misc. Notes:

Have your student draw a picture or write a reflection on the Bible verse(s) in the space below.

Five in a Row Bible Supplement 35

Angelo

The tale of *Angelo* by David Macaulay reminds us of the story in the Bible of the **Good Samaritan**. In the Bible story, a man who has been traveling from Jerusalem (probably a Jewish man) is robbed and beaten. Another man, a Samaritan, finds him and gives him first aid, as well as taking him to a place of recuperation and paying for it himself. Between the Jews and the Samaritans there was not only "professional dislike" but religious and cultural dislike as well. Nevertheless, the Samaritan man took good care of the man who was hurt just like Angelo took good care of Sylvia, even though he didn't even like pigeons! You can read the story of the Good Samaritan in Luke 10:30-37 and find that the Lord wants us to be full of mercy for the suffering of others in the same way that He, Himself is merciful. He says this will help us be good neighbors. Colossians 3:12 also shows us to have a heart filled with compassion.

Luke 10:30-37

Colossians 3:12

Matthew 21:28-32

In Matthew 21:28-32 there is also the **parable of the two sons**. In this parable Jesus talks about a son who was asked to do a task. He said he would, but then he did not do it. The second son, when asked, said he did not want to, but later he regretted his decision and did the work. Angelo is like the second son, who really did not want to do the work of caring for Sylvia. He grumbles that he is a repairer of buildings not pigeons. He tries very hard to find someone else to do the job, but when he cannot he gives first aid and a compassionate home to the injured creature. Though he begins the task of mercy with an "I don't want to be doing this," attitude, he finishes the job creatively and with great care. Interestingly enough Angleo reaps great rewards of friendship with Sylvia in the end.

When Angelo knew he was so old and tired that he was about to die, he was worried. What worried him? He wanted to know that Sylvia would be cared for. This is what parents feel about their children—they want to **care for them** and provide safe environments and homes. You can see this type of care in the early scenes of Jesus' life as Mary gives birth in the stable (Luke 2:6-7). And, as Moses' mother carefully makes the reed basket to keep him safe (Exodus 2:1-10), as the boy's mother packs loaves of bread and fish for his lunch (John 6:8-10), but most of all in all the provisions that God the Father has made for us in the work of His Son Jesus Christ, and in all the ways he cares for us each day.

Luke 2:6-7
Exodus 2:1-10
John 6:8-10

Does your student remember the line of the story where is says that Angelo looked carefully over the walls of the building for cracks? It says that he would have to repair these cracks before he applied the stucco. Did your student ever think what would happen to the beautiful buildings if Angelo did not have a good work ethic or **integrity**? What if when no one was looking, Angelo just applied the stucco over the cracked walls? He could say he had done his job but what would the results be? The stucco would soon crack and the work would have to be redone. Has your student ever heard the saying about not sweeping dirt under the rug? Obviously this saying came about because some people would go to the trouble to sweep a room but not bend down to pick up the debris. Instead they would just sweep the dirt under the rug when no one was looking as a lazy shortcut to their work. (This saying has since come to mean hiding anything that you don't want people to see and forgetting about it. But, in whatever context, the saying carries the concept of lack of integrity.) The Bible has a verse encouraging believers to do their work well remembering that they are doing it for the Lord (Colossians 3:17). Isn't it wonderful that Angelo was an honest man, full of pride in his work and with enough integrity to do his work well?

Colossians 3:17

Teacher's Notes

The *Teacher's Notes* are optional but provide a space for you to document which Bible verse you choose and any other discussion points, songs, verses or notes you wish to keep record of for your student.

ANGELO

Date:

Student:

Five in a Row Bible Verse(s):

☐ Memorized Verse(s) / Copywork

Character Trait or Life Lesson to apply:

Related Worship Songs/Hymns

Misc. Notes:

Have your student draw a picture or write a reflection on the Bible verse(s) in the space below.

Paper Lanterns

Since the word **lamp** is a synonym for lantern, a good verse to have in mind during the time you read *Paper Lanterns* would be Psalm 119:105 This verse speaks about God's Word being the very light we must have to walk through this world in safety. What a wonderful verse to remember as we study lanterns!

Psalm 119:105

Paper Lanterns reminds us of the story of **David** and how he was chosen from all his brothers to be anointed King by the prophet Samuel (1 Samuel 16:1-13). Remember that David was the youngest son, still tending the sheep on the hillside (not a glamorous job in those days). One after another, Samuel thought each of Jesse's other sons was the one to be anointed King, and each time the Lord said no. Finally, Jesse said he had one more son, the littlest (youngest) and when David was sent for, the Lord said, "Arise, anoint him, for this is he."

1 Samuel 16:1-13

We often think of the young David being brave and courageous and passionate about God's name, and taking down the giant Goliath. In this story, the youngest boy, Little Mouse, was the one who, by his passion, took down the "snideness sent his way." Little Mouse became the one to take over the work, becoming like Old Chen, the master craftsman and owner.

Does your student understand that when he is able to turn his back on poor behavior of others toward him, and keep cheerful, it is like David taking down the giant? In both cases, for David as for your student, it takes the help of God to do God's work.

As Little Mouse puts himself under Mr. Chen's care and instruction, he spends more and more time with the artist/teacher. He listens to stories, shares meals, watches carefully to see exactly how the old lantern maker does his work. Little Mouse goes home and practices what he has observed. He practices over and over. He listens and listens. Then we read the line in the story: "The apprentices were surprised at how much Little Mouse acted and sounded like Old Chen."

One thing comes to mind as we read about **putting one's self under a teacher**, and that is that we need to choose the teacher that not only knows his trade or craft, but also has integrity and Christian values. We want a teacher that will be good for us to be like.

Luke 6:27-49 — This reminds us of a verse in the Bible about the followers of Jesus. Together with your student, read Luke 6 beginning at verse 27, through the end of the chapter. There are several parts of this reading that tie in beautifully to *Paper Lanterns*. The verses about loving your enemies, as well as the commandment to love one's neighbor also help keep us on the right track when people are not being kind to us.

Luke 6:40 — Luke 6:40 is about a student not being above his teacher (that's asking for respect) but when trained is like his teacher, fits perfectly with the Little Mouse/Old Chen scenario. It is even more important when it also covers children/parents, or His followers/Jesus!

The Bible has a lot to say about being **humble**. Acting out of fear that you will not be valued as much as you think you ought to be, or that you will lose your spot to someone else, can result is some rather ugly behavior. Words spoken such as "I'm the only one," or commands like "you must" are not helpful in the workplace. Seeing the situation for what it is and making a choice to be respectful and kind and let your own giftings make room for you is the best way to handle this sort of fear.

Proverbs 18:16 — Proverbs 18:16 is good to remember: "A man's gift makes room for him and brings him before the great." This way we can put our fears to rest, and let the Lord put us where we should be.

In our story the apprentices may have felt superior to Little Mouse, and perhaps they also wanted to be sure they wouldn't lose their particular place in the shop. In the Bible, the Pharisees were worried that Jesus would take their place. What they failed completely to realize was that in their case Jesus *was* the Master and they had taken *His* place.

When we look at how Jesus came to rescue us, it is clear that being humble is an integral part of who He is. He came as a helpless human baby, had no palace in which to rest His head, rode on a donkey instead of prancing stallions, washed the feet of His pupils, and suffered innocently a violent death. He did not brag or show off (He often left quickly after doing a supernatural act)—all this He did, even though He had created all things and had "been" since the beginning. This is our King, this is the one we are to follow and the Master we want to look like. Being willing to be humble is important!

The Bible says in Proverbs 27:1-2 not to **boast** about tomorrow because we don't know exactly what we'll be doing, and to let someone else praise us, not our own lips. Who were the two characters in the story that did not follow this Proverb? Did they end up looking rather foolish for their boasting?

Proverbs 27:1-2

There are many other verses of the Bible that teach us about the consequences of boasting. Paul said while he could say much, he wanted to boast only in Jesus and what Jesus has done (Galatians 6:14).

Galatians 6:14

Little Mouse was **persistent**. At first he kept coming by the lantern shop, feasting his eyes on the amazing creations. Little Mouse began to ask Old Chen if he could become one of Mr. Chen's apprentices, and the lantern maker always said, "No you are still too small." But Little Mouse did not give up, and finally one day Old Chen said, "All right, Little Mouse, I will give you work. You can sweep the shop for me." Little Mouse was finally in the door!

In Luke 11:5-13, Jesus is teaching what prayer is like. He says that it it is good to be intentional and persistent about our times of coming to the Lord and asking for things. We can ask and keep asking, keep knocking, and keep seeking until we receive the Lord's answer, whatever that answer may be.

Luke 11:5-13

Teacher's Notes

The *Teacher's Notes* are optional but provide a space for you to document which Bible verse you choose and any other discussion points, songs, verses or notes you wish to keep record of for your student.

PAPER LANTERNS

Date: _____

Student: _____

Five in a Row Bible Verse(s):

_____
_____
_____
_____
_____
_____
_____

☐ Memorized Verse(s) / Copywork

Character Trait or Life Lesson to apply:

_____
_____
_____

Related Worship Songs/Hymns

_____
_____
_____
_____
_____

Misc. Notes:

_____
_____
_____
_____
_____
_____
_____
_____

Have your student draw a picture or write a reflection on the Bible verse(s) in the space below.

The Bravest of Us All

One of the shinning moments in *The Bravest of Us All* is at the end when Velma Jean gives Ruby Jane credit for being brave.

Ask your student if he knows that in the Bible there are many instances of someone being highly commended for what they have done? Jesus was wonderful about **giving sincere credit** when someone had done something special. Here just a few of the instances where you and your student can compare what Velma Jean did and what Jesus does.

In Matthew 8, Jesus told the people around him that he was amazed at the great faith displayed by the Roman soldier. Jesus stopped what he was doing to draw attention to this particular soldier and what he had done!

Matthew 8:5-13

In Matthew 26 there is a story of a woman who took something precious and valuable to her and gave it to Jesus. The people around her complained that she had wasted it. Jesus had a different look, a look into her heart, and told them it was fine. But he didn't stop there, He made sure she received the credit for her generous action for a long time!

Matthew 26:6-13

In Luke 21:1-4 you can read about a woman who put some of her coins in the temple offering place. The Bible says she is a widow and yet she is there making her offering among the others. Apparently Jesus see her and tells his disciples that he recognizes that she has actually put in more than the rich people did, because she has given not just a little, but everything she had! He draws attention to her and gives her credit for her actions.

Luke 21:1-4

As you read the Bible watch for instances where credit is given when it is due. Just as the Lord has demonstrated for us how to do this, so we ought to look for opportunities to give credit where credit is due!

Ruby Jane tells Velma Jean that she will not go to safety unless her sister comes, too. In effect, she is **laying down her own safety (or life)** for another. The Bible tells us that a willingness to lay down one's life for another is a sign of love or friendship (John 10:11, John 15:13, 1 John 3:16). Jesus, Himself, was the best example ever of this and you can certainly explore this analogy with your student.

John 10:11
John 15:13
1 John 3:16

Five in a Row Bible Supplement

Esther With your older student, you might want to read through the book of Esther. Re-tell the story briefly and stress the moment when Esther decides she will lay down her own life in an attempt to save the lives of her people. Esther says that she will seek out the King, though he has not called for her, and she says, "If I perish, I perish." (Esther 4:16b) It does remind us of Ruby Jane's declaration, "I'm not going without you!"

1 Samuel 17 David the young shepherd was willing to take on Goliath in an effort that was both the willingness to face the possibility of laying down his life as well as exhibiting bravery as he trusted in God.

There are numerous examples of people laying down their lives for others through out the Bible. Have your student watch for these instances as he hears more and more of the Scriptures.

Ruby Jane finally gets Velma Jean into the storm cellar just in time. But Velma Jean is uncomfortable and feels closed in underground. Ruby Jane lets her feel the warm egg, and see the buttons, and tries to **comfort** her as best she can until they can all come up out of the cellar.

There are dozens of instances of the word "comfort" in the Bible. Ask your student why he thinks that is. Why do people so often turn to the Bible for comfort, just as Velma Jean needed comfort when she was afraid? Use this opportunity to show your student how to use a Bible concordance (in print or online), or how to use Bible Gateway or another Bible app and search for the word "comfort." Read through several verses with your student and notice how this word is found throughout the Bible, from beginning to end.

Proverbs 17:17
Colossians 3:14 One verse in particular sums up the truth that we find in *The Bravest of Us All*: Proverbs 17:17. In this case it was a sister, but she came through in times of adversity! A related verse is Colossians 3:14, which speaks of love being the perfect bond of unity.

In *The Bravest of Us All* there was **water** in Cowskin Creek, more water in the stock tank, and water coming down from the storm. Are there other places in the story where your student can find water?

It reminds us of the time Moses parted the waters (Exodus 14), and when he struck the rock to get water (Numbers 20:10-12).

Exodus 14
Numbers 20:10-12

Jeremiah 17:8 talks about a tree planted by the waters and how well that tree grew!

Jeremiah 17:8

Jesus said that He was the Living Water. Read the story of the woman at the well and re-tell it for your student (John 4:10-11).

John 4:10-11

Jesus went on to say that whoever believed in Him would have living water (John 7:38).

John 7:38

And even in Revelation 7:17 it says there will be springs of living water!

Revelation 7:17

There are hundreds of verses that speak of water, from the waters of the Flood, to the baptisms, spring rains, latter rains, etc. Enjoy finding verses that speak of water as you continue to read through Scripture with your student.

Ruby Jane brought up vegetable from the root cellar and helped her mother bake bread, but she said that sometimes supper was a mite meager and that's when they took off to eat the sandhill plums. This might be a good opportunity to talk with your student about not always having everything he wants, but rather being happy (or **content**) with all that he does have.

Philippians 4:11-12

Teacher's Notes

The *Teacher's Notes* are optional but provide a space for you to document which Bible verse you choose and any other discussion points, songs, verses or notes you wish to keep record of for your student.

THE BRAVEST OF US ALL

Date: _____

Student: _____

Five in a Row Bible Verse(s):

_____
_____
_____
_____
_____
_____
_____
_____

☐ Memorized Verse(s) / Copywork

Character Trait or Life Lesson to apply:

_____
_____
_____

Related Worship Songs/Hymns

_____
_____
_____
_____
_____

Misc. Notes:

_____
_____
_____
_____
_____
_____
_____
_____
_____
_____

Have your student draw a picture or write a reflection on the Bible verse(s) in the space below.

The Hatmaker's Sign

Remind your student that Thomas Jefferson wrote words that sang. He felt his words were the best words for the project at hand. Then make the connection that there is a very special book of words. Does your student know what that is? It's the Bible, God's words to His people. Each of the following verses also has to do with "**words**."

- Psalm 119, verses 11 and 105.
- John 1:1 reminds us that in the beginning was the Word (Jesus).
- John 6:68, where Simon Peter tells Jesus that Jesus has the words of eternal life.
- John 8:31, Jesus says that if people would abide in His Word that they would be his disciples.
- Romans 10:17, another reference to the Word of Christ.
- Galatians 5:14, how is the whole law fulfilled in one "word?"
- 2 Timothy 2: 15 is an admonishment to be careful to study the Word so that you can handle it accurately.
- Hebrews 4:12, the Word of God is living and active and compared to a two-edged sword.
- James 1:22 reminds us to be doers of the Word and not merely hearers.
- 1 John 1:1, John's testimony about being with the one (Jesus) who was the Word of Life.

Psalm 119:11 & 105
John 1:1
John 6:68

John 8:31

Romans 10:17
Galatians 5:14
2 Timothy 2:15

Hebrews 4:12

James 1:22
1 John 1:1

Compassion and sympathy are demonstrated by Benjamin Franklin, when, like a good friend, he tries to **comfort** Jefferson. In 2 Corinthians 1:3-4 it says that God is the God of all comfort, who comforts us so that we can comfort others with the same comfort that we have received.

2 Corinthians 1:3-4

After running all over town, John was exhausted. This reminds us of what Jesus said in Matthew 11:28-30—that He wanted all to come to Him that were weary and He would **give them rest**.

Matthew 11:28-30

Jefferson was struggling with some **pride** issues. He thought his words were best and was upset that anyone would want to change them. This feeling, apparently (from information in the Author's Note at the back of the *The Hatmaker's Sign*), never left him and he was bothered by it for the rest of his life. Perhaps some

Romans 12:3 Micah 6:8 1 Corinthians 8:1	of these verses might have helped him: Romans 12:3, Micah 6:8 about being humble, and the last sentence of 1 Corinthians 8:1 about how knowledge puffs us up while love edifies.
1 Samuel 17 Daniel 6 Daniel 3	As John hurries all over town, he meets the magistrate who speaks in an intimidating manner, "Hand it over or face the stockades!" David, in the story of David and Goliath in 1 Samuel 17, Daniel in Daniel 6, and Shadrach, Meshach and Abednego in Daniel 3, all faced intimidating circumstances and stood up for what they believed. There are some extreme circumstances that call for this kind of courage.
Romans 13:1-10	But many intimidating circumstances are less critical and the believer, armed with the knowledge of who he is in God, can let these situations go with a soft answer. The magistrate is not asking John to compromise his faith, though the magistrate is cruel in the way he asks for what he wants. Thus, John carries out the verses of Romans 13:1-10 as he graciously submits to the governing authority even though the man is intimidating.
Micah 6:8 Galatians 5:22-23	Some of the clues we receive to John's **polite and respectful character** are that he listens to his wife, tips his hat to the Reverend, kisses the gloved hand of the Lady (as the respectful behavior of the day), lawfully hands over to magistrate the paper and bows to him, and generously gives the boy apprentices some money. Micah 6:8 tells us what God would like us to do, while Galatians 5:22-23 reminds us of the fruit of the Spirit which we grow in as we abide closely with the Lord.

Teacher's Notes

The *Teacher's Notes* are optional but provide a space for you to document which Bible verse you choose and any other discussion points, songs, verses or notes you wish to keep record of for your student.

THE HATMAKER'S SIGN

Date:

Student:

Five in a Row Bible Verse(s):

☐ Memorized Verse(s) / Copywork

Character Trait or Life Lesson to apply:

Related Worship Songs/Hymns

Misc. Notes:

Have your student draw a picture or write a reflection on the Bible verse(s) in the space below.

Thomas A. Edison: Young Inventor

Chapter 1—An Idea That Didn't Work

Tom Edison was sure he knew what would make those goslings hatch. Why didn't it work? God's creation is so **complex and unexplainable**! The human mind can understand only so much. Tom knew it took warmth for the eggs to hatch, but he didn't know why. The Bible tells us to trust in God and not depend on our own knowledge (Proverbs 3:5). Does this mean we should never experiment and try to understand nature? Of course not. But the Lord doesn't want us to become frustrated trying to figure everything out. Some things are unexplainable. The following verses discuss what our Heavenly Father knows and understands: Psalms 44:21 and 94:11, Matthew 6:8, and 2 Timothy 2:19. The Lord is an awesome Being who created all and knows all!

Proverbs 3:5
Psalm 44:21
Psalm 94:11
Matthew 6:8
2 Timothy 2:19

Chapter 2—Tom Visits the Shipyards

In the second chapter of our book, Tom saw Sandy spreading **pitch** on a barge. Does your student know that the Bible talks about pitch? Take this opportunity to recount the amazing story of Noah and his ark. In Genesis 6:14, God tells Noah how to build his ark. He tells him to make it out of cypress wood and cover it all over with pitch. He even tells him the exact dimensions the ark should be! The story of Noah and the flood which covered the earth is incredible, not only because of the great waters and animals and ark, but because of God's promise in the rainbow to never flood the earth again. The next time your student sees a rainbow, remind her to think about God's loving promise, Noah, his ark and the pitch! (Exodus 2:3, which describes how Moses' mother hid her baby son in a basket, has another reference to pitch.)

Genesis 6:14

Exodus 2:3

Chapter 3—A Birthday to Remember

Tom didn't **obey** Sandy's careful instructions on the ice. If he had listened, he wouldn't have fallen in the canal and risked being seriously injured. God cares about us so much, He gives us rules and laws to obey so we will be safe. He knows this world can be dangerous and confusing.

The Bible tells us that we can determine if we know God by how we do at obeying His commands (1 John 2:3). Sometimes, obeying isn't easy! Tom was so excited to be skating he didn't listen to Sandy. It is simple to get distracted or caught up in our own thinking! Look over the following verses and think about how we as Christians need to hold God's precepts close to our hearts and obey them: Deuteronomy 6:25, Psalm 119:57 and 119:167, Colossians 3:20, 2 John 6.

1 John 2:3

Deuteronomy 6:25
Psalm 119:57 & 167
Colossians 3:20
2 John 6

Chapter 4—Off For a New Home

The Edisons had to plan long and hard for their **move** to Michigan. Moving a family of four takes a lot of work! Share with your student the story of Moses and the Israelites in the wilderness. Imagine planning a cross-country move for thousands and thousands of people! Talk with your student about the logistics—food, shelter and clothes needed. There weren't any moving vans at that time. How would you carry your things? What things could you take? What about the little children who couldn't walk that far? How would you plan for an enormous move like this? In the book of Numbers, chapter 14, the Bible tells the story of the people's complaints against God and their punishment—40 years of wandering through the desert! Now that is a long move! God was still with the Israelites however, and through the long, difficult journey He met them.

Numbers 14

Chapter 5—Tom's First Train Ride

It took a great deal of boldness and **confidence** for Tom to approach Mr. Benjamin and ask him questions about the train! Tom even asked if he could ride with the old engineer. Confidence and boldness are two characteristics the Bible says we should have when we approach the Lord in prayer. In Hebrews 4:16, the Bible tells us to approach the Lord's throne in confidence to ask for help when we need it. Our Heavenly Father does not want us to be shy or frightened by Him. He desires us to run to Him and talk, just like Tom did with Mr. Benjamin.

Hebrews 4:16

In Proverbs 28:1, we read that the righteous should be bold, like a lion. Encourage one another to seek out the Lord and talk with Him, without fear and timidity. He created and loves us—surely we can ask Him anything!

Proverbs 28:1

Five in a Row Bible Supplement

Chapter 6—The House in the Grove

The Edisons' new **neighbors** were very kind to clean the new home before their arrival. The Bible talks about the importance of being kind to strangers and neighbors, alike. Look at Proverbs 3:28-29 with your student. This Scripture tells us to give our neighbors what they need and to trust them. Learning to live in peace with one another is an important life skill. Encourage your student to replicate this Biblical principle in her own life and study the following verses which talk about neighbors and caring: Matthew 19:19, Luke 10:27, Acts 7:26-27 and Romans 13:10.

Proverbs 3:28-29

Matthew 19:19
Luke 10:27
Acts 7:26-27
Romans 13:10

Chapter 7—First Day at School

Tom was wrong to ignore Mr. Crawford's lessons in class. It is easy to become distracted or bored, but learning to **respect** our elders and people in authority is important. The Bible talks about this very thing in Hebrews 13:17. The Lord tells us to obey our leaders and those who are in authority. Encourage your student to cultivate this respect in his own life with those in authority around him. In Leviticus 19:32 God tells His children to show respect for the elderly and to show respect for Him. When we conduct ourselves in this manner, we not only glorify God, but we reap the benefits of a life consistent with His Word!

Hebrews 13:17

Leviticus 19:32

Chapter 8—The Basement Laboratory

Tom is embarrassed and hurt by Mr. Crawford's treatment of him. Tom is different from the other children, but to make fun of him is unnecessary. The Bible teaches us to have **mercy** on those around us and show them compassion, care and love. In the book of Jude, the words tell us to be merciful to others. In fact, it tells us to snatch them from the fire and save them!

Jude 21-23

When we are faced with someone who is different from us (perhaps an intellectual, religious, racial or social difference), it is our special commission from God to treat them with respect and care, not to shame them or make them feel uneasy. With the same gentle love Jesus shows us, so we should share with others!

Chapter 9—Tom Tries an Experiment

Tom and Michael's garden yields a bountiful harvest! The Bible has many stories about **planting and reaping**. Share with your student one or several of the following examples. In Mark 4:1-9, Jesus shares the parable of the sower. This important tale examines the nature of our hearts as listeners to God's Word. If the seed of His Word lands on good soil (soft, humble hearts), it will yield much fruit. If we harden our hearts and minds to God, His seed will fall on rocky soil.

Mark 4:1-9

In Ecclesiastes 3:2, the Bible tells us there is a time to plant and a time to uproot. In our lives, just like a garden, we will have seasons of steady growth and seasons of change.

Ecclesiastes 3:2

Encourage your student to look up these two verses, as well as the following references, and remember to think about Tom and his carefully tended garden: Matthew 9:37, John 4:35, Galatians 6:9 and Hebrews 12:11.

Matthew 9:37
John 4:35
Galatians 6:9
Hebrews 12:11

Chapter 10— Tom's First Telegraph

Tom's family lived very near Fort Gratiot. Talk with your student about what a **fort** is like—high walls, protecting towers, safety for the soldiers, security, a refuge, a source of food and shelter, etc. During a war, having a strong fortress is important. The Bible describes God as our fortress. Life is sometimes difficult and we often feel as if we are in a war. When you are tired and weary, remember the Lord can be your strength. Read the following verses and discuss with your student how she can trust in the Lord to be her safe place—her fort: 2 Samuel 22:2, Psalms 18:2, 31:3, 71:3, 91:2, 144:2, and Jeremiah 16:19a.

2 Samuel 22:2
Psalm 18:2
Psalm 31:3
Psalm 71:3
Psalm 91:2
Psalm 144:2
Jeremiah 16:19a

Chapter 11—A Job on a Train

Tom works very hard at home and soon he will begin a new job on the train! What does it take to be a **hard worker**? If we practice diligence and care, we will ensure a good beginning! The Bible tells us God watches our efforts and remembers our diligence (Hebrews 6:10-11). He won't forget what He sees in us and will reward us for persevering. The key to being diligent at our work is to

Hebrews 6:10-11

Five in a Row Bible Supplement

remember who we are doing it for—our employer (or mom and dad), ourselves (working hard makes us feel good inside) and most importantly, the Lord! When we work hard at a job and do it well, we honor our Maker. Working hard and cheerfully is our way of saying "thank you" to God for all He has given to us.

Chapter 12—The Underground Railway

2 Peter 2:19

Tom is aware that Finney's Hotel is used as a stop for the Underground Railroad—a resting place for **slaves** who are seeking freedom. 2 Peter 2:19 speaks of another kind of slavery—that people can be slaves to whatever masters them. What does that mean?

Whenever we submit to being angry, jealous, spiteful, lying or any other ungodly characteristic, then we are no longer free, but a slave to our behavior. Unlike the slaves in early America, however, we have a choice. Each time we choose to be loving, honoring, compassionate, joyful, etc., our "chains" are loosened and we become more free in God. What a wonderful thing! The more we emulate (try to be like) our Heavenly Father, the more liberated we become!

Chapter 13—The Laboratory on Wheels

Tom is anxious to work on his inventions. But how can he sell papers all day (a job which must be done) and still have time to work with his chemicals? Tom gets a wonderful idea. If he were to move his laboratory onto the train and **delegate** some of his selling responsibilities to his friend James, he could then work on his own projects. The Bible has a very similar story.

Acts 6:1-7

In Acts 6:1-7, the Word tells us the disciples grew frustrated. They knew they should be taking meals to the widows and orphans, but at the same time they needed to be busy preaching the Gospel. They had a similar idea to Tom's! Instead of neglecting either important calling, they chose a few men who were godly and full of wisdom and delegated the feeding of the widows to them. In that way, all tasks could be completed.

If Tom had spent all his time selling papers, he might never have been able to become the scientist and inventor we know him as today. Little did he know, however, that he was exercising a Biblical principle when he hired James to help him!

Chapter 14—Tom's Own Newspaper

The main topic of Tom's newspaper was the Civil War. People wanted to know about recent battles and their outcomes. War is certainly not a modem concept. In fact, you can share with your student some stories from the Bible about historic **battles** that were fought. The Bible (and all of history) is filled with stories of warring nations and peoples.

One such story is found in 1 Samuel, chapter 17. Share with your student this wonderful story of a young boy named David, son of Jesse.

1 Samuel 17

We find the Philistines gathered to fight the Israelites. Every day for 40 days, the Philistines had sent Goliath, their biggest warrior, to the front lines to see if any of the Israelites would fight him. No one comes forward until David says he will take on the giant. Imagine! A young boy going to fight this enormous mountain of a man! But the Lord was with David and the miracle of how the fight ends attests to David's favor with God.

Another great story of battle is found in the book of Joshua, chapter 6. Read with your student the amazing victory over Jericho as the Lord helped Joshua and his men. Also in this story is the touching story of Rahab and how the Lord protected her family in the midst of the battle.

Joshua 6

God is an amazing warrior. He plans strategies no human could ever have conceived and carries them out in His perfect timing.

Chapter 15—An Explosion

Tom is sure he has his chemistry set securely fastened on the shelf. Most importantly, he has tried his best to safely secure his dangerous stick of phosphorus.

Five in a Row Bible Supplement

But what happens? The train hits a rough section of track and lurches back and forth, spilling the contents of Tom's shelves onto the floor and starting a fire. Did Tom know this accident was going to happen? Of course not. Nor do we know when difficult times are going to hit us.

Matthew 7:24-27
Luke 6:46-49

Share with your student the parable of the **wise and foolish builders** (Matthew 7:24-27 or Luke 6:46-49). We must build strong foundations in the Lord to withstand unexpected storms in life. The more wisely we build our life in God, the better prepared we will be when we traverse "rough track." Encourage your student to sink deep roots in God!

Chapter 16—Moving Pictures

Tom's paper dolls "danced" next to the static electricity. **Dancing** is a form of movement which can express a wide range of emotions. The Bible tells many stories of people dancing. For example, you may want to share with your student

2 Samuel 6:16

the story found in 2 Samuel 6:16. In this account, we find the man after God's own heart, King David, awaiting the arrival of the ark of the covenant. When he sees the holy ark, the Bible tells us he danced before the Lord with all his might! Imagine a king and ruler dancing like that! David told his wife, who was embarrassed by his actions, that he wasn't ashamed before the Lord and he wanted to celebrate!

Psalm 149:3
Psalm 150:4
Ecclesiastes 3:4
Lamentations 5:15
Exodus 15:20

That same man, David, wrote many of the psalms we find in the Bible. In Psalms 149:3 and 150:4, the Bible tells us to praise the Lord's name with dance. Here are some more references to dance: Ecclesiastes 3:4, Lamentations 5:15, Exodus 15:20.

Chapter 17—Light's Golden Jubilee

Thomas Edison invents a wonderful thing—the light bulb! Can you imagine life today without it? Light bulbs help illuminate our lives every day. Does your student know that Jesus described himself in terms of **light**?

In John 8:12, Jesus speaks to the questioning disciples and He tells them that He is the Light of the world! Jesus also says that whoever will follow Him shall never walk in darkness. In 1 John 1:5, the Bible tells us that God is light. No matter how big it is, someday every light bulb burns out. God's light, however, will never diminish. It is eternal and fills the world! Share with your student other verses which talk about the light of God: John 1:3-4, Psalms 27:1, 56:13, 104:2, Isaiah 2:5, 2 Corinthians 4:6.

John 8:12
1 John 1:5
John 1:3-4
Psalm 27:1
Psalm 56:13
Psalm 104:2
Isaiah 2:5
2 Corinthians 4:6

Five in a Row Bible Supplement

Teacher's Notes

The *Teacher's Notes* are optional but provide a space for you to document which Bible verse you choose and any other discussion points, songs, verses or notes you wish to keep record of for your student.

THOMAS A. EDISON: YOUNG INVENTOR

Date:

Student:

Five in a Row Bible Verse(s):

☐ Memorized Verse(s) / Copywork

Character Trait or Life Lesson to apply:

Related Worship Songs/Hymns

Misc. Notes:

Have your student draw a picture or write a reflection on the Bible verse(s) in the space below.

Sarah, Plain and Tall

Chapter 1

Mr. Jacob Witting, Anna and Caleb's Papa, placed an advertisement for a new wife. He most assuredly missed the companionship of a woman, and he knew his children longed for a mama to care for them. The Bible talks about **marriage** and being alone. In Genesis 2:18, God created the first woman and named her Eve. The Bible tells us after He had created Adam, God said, "It is not good that the man should be alone." God knows how much we need others for support, love and help. Just as Adam needed Eve, Jacob needs Sarah.

Genesis 2:18

God always knows what is best for us. He planned on a **family** including a mother and a father. Sometimes, sad or trying times come, and we find ourselves without a father, mother or both. Even then, the Lord promises in Psalm 146:9 that He will be a father to the fatherless. Families come in many shapes and sizes. Because of different circumstances, sometimes a family is just a father and his children, like Papa, Anna and Caleb. Sometimes, it is only a mother and her children. Or just siblings, with no parents at all. However, through God's love, we can all experience happiness, fullness and joy with our family—no matter what it looks like. Always remember, God knows what you need before you do. If you are lacking, He is always sufficient.

Psalm 146:9

Chapter 2

Sarah gives the children an introduction to herself through her letters. She knows they wonder what she is like and she describes herself in interesting detail. Does your student know that God does the same thing for us in His Word? He tells us many things about Himself and about Jesus throughout the Bible. He wants us to know what He is like, who He is. Just like a good friend, He is always willing to give us new insights into His characteristics and ways— even His many names.

In Isaiah 9:6, we see four of Jesus' many names: Wonderful Counselor, Mighty God, Everlasting Father and Prince of Peace. Even His names describe Him more for us, don't they?

Isaiah 9:6

Five in a Row Bible Supplement

Psalm 91:4
Psalm 121:5
Proverbs 3:12
Hebrews 10:23
1 John 1:9
1 John 4:19
Revelation 19:11-16

Take some time and look at the following passages for more insight and an introduction, like Sarah's introduction, to our Heavenly Father and His Son: Psalms 91:4, 121:5, Proverbs 3:12, Hebrews 10:23, 1 John 1:9, 1 John 4:19, Revelation 19:11-16.

Chapter 3

Anna and Caleb watched expectantly down the road for Sarah and Papa to return. When Caleb spotted the yellow bonnet, he shouted with excitement. There is a story in the Bible about a similar situation. Share with your student the tale of the prodigal son. In this story, the father misses his son greatly. Jesus tells us (Luke 15:20) that when the son returns home, his father is watching for him. We know this because the Bible says, "...while he [the son] was still a long way off, his father saw him ..." He was watching for his lost son—just as Caleb and Anna watched for Sarah to arrive.

Luke 15:20

With the same longing of a father whose son is lost, so our Heavenly Father yearns to see us. Even while we are still lost, His eyes search the horizon for our safe return home. We are precious in His sight and just as the father runs towards his son, so God will run toward us.

Chapter 4

Sarah, Anna and Caleb collect beautiful flowers for drying. That is one way to preserve the color, but the flower still fades and it dies. In Isaiah 40:8, we see this issue addressed. In fact, the Lord contrasts His Word to a flower. He says that grasses and flowers will wither and fade, but His Word will stand forever. No matter how much we wish a beautiful wild rose could last, we know it will eventually die.

Isaiah 40:8

But we can rest in the knowledge that the Lord and His Word are eternal. They don't grow old or weary or even fade. Forever the Lord will be our Father and His words will guide and protect us. And by being Christians, children of God, we also can be with Him for eternity. What a wonderful, loving God we serve!

Chapter 5

When the children, Papa and Sarah go out to the barn to slide down their dune, it is dark and the **stars** are already making their appearance. Has your student ever tried to count the stars? It is impossible! The celestial objects overhead are far too numerous to count. In the Bible, the Lord made a very special promise to a man named Abram (Abraham). It was a very serious promise, called a covenant. Abram was very sad because he had no children. But the Lord had specific plans for Abram and his family. The Lord, in fact, told Abram (Genesis 15:5) to look up at the stars. Abram does, and the Lord asks him if he can count them. Then the Lord makes a covenant with Abram. He tells him, by faith, that he will have more descendants than the stars—more than he could ever imagine. That must have been difficult for Abram to believe, since he did not even have one child with his wife, Sarah. But Abram believed the Lord—and it came to pass! Remember, the Lord never breaks a covenant or promise to His children. He will never fail you!

Genesis 15:5

Chapter 6

Sarah leads the children to the cow pond and teaches them to swim. What fun! And imagine how delightful that must have been on a hot summer day. The Lord understands how refreshing **water** can be when we are thirsty and tired. In Psalm 23:2, He promises to lead us by the cool streams. In Isaiah 49:10 the Bible tells us our Heavenly Father will lead us beside streams of water. When we are spiritually dry and thirsty, our spirits crave the refreshment of God's Word—just as our bodies grow weary. Remind your student of the Lord's refreshing qualities and His promise (Isaiah 58:11) to calm our dry, cracked souls with water from the greatest spring of all—Himself!

Psalm 23:2
Isaiah 49:10

Isaiah 58:11

Chapter 7

Maggie was a wonderful **neighbor** to Sarah. She brought food and helped Sarah provide the meal for the families. She assisted in the manual work (harnessing up the horses and planting the garden). But most importantly, she provided a listening ear and understanding heart. She cared for Sarah and made her feel

Five in a Row Bible Supplement

Leviticus 19:13
Leviticus 19:18
Proverbs 27:10b
Luke 10:27-29

better. The Bible has a lot to say about neighbors. Jesus teaches that we should love our neighbors as we love ourselves. When we are kind to others, we are acting in a way that is pleasing to God. Share with your student some of these "neighbor" verses, and plan on doing a kind deed for a neighbor today: Leviticus 19:13, 19:18, Proverbs 27:10b, Luke 10:27-29.

Chapter 8

Anna, Papa, Sarah and Caleb are shut tight away in the barn throughout the squall. The animals are with them as well—Seal, the chickens, Nick, Lottie and the horses. What would it be like to spend all night long in a darkened barn with all those animals while a storm raged outside? Noah, a man in the Bible, had a similar experience. Read with your student the story of **Noah and the ark** found in Genesis 7:1-24. The Lord told Noah that He was angry with the rebellion of the people in the world. He wanted to destroy the earth with a flood and begin again, but He recognized Noah's faithfulness to Him and wished to save Noah and his family. God also wanted to preserve the animals on the earth so they would be able to multiply and fill the earth again, after the floods subsided.

Genesis 7:1-24

Noah obeyed the Lord and built a huge boat, called an ark. The word ark comes from the Latin *arca*, meaning box. God gave Noah specific dimensions for the ark: 450 feet long, 45 feet high and 75 feet wide. When the storms came, Noah was ready. He and his family, all the animals and enough supplies for everyone were on the ark and they remained there. Imagine—being in a floating "box" with all those animals while a storm is raging outside! The storm itself, the Bible tells us, lasted 40 days and 40 nights, but the floods persisted for almost five months! But the Lord saved Noah, just as He said He would.

Chapter 9

Caleb and Anna are frightened that Sarah **might leave them**. Caleb even thinks of ways to prevent her from going. When Jesus lived on the earth, His disciples became close friends with Him. They knew He was the Messiah and when He was crucified, they were devastated. But we know that three days later, Jesus rose again, victorious (Matthew 28:1-10). Surely the disciples hoped He would

Matthew 28:1-10

stay with them from then on. They probably wondered why He was leaving again—to go back to Heaven to be with His Father. But, in a wonderful way, Jesus promised He would never "leave" them and would be with them always.

Now known as the "Great Commission," Jesus told them what He wanted His followers to do on Earth when He left (Matthew 28:16-20). He asked the disciples (and us, as Christians) to make disciples of the nations and to teach others to obey His ways. Then He said He would be with us "always, to the end of the age." What a comforting message for our hearts! Caleb and Anna have nothing to worry about. Sarah is coming back. And we should never worry, either. Our Father is with us always!

Matthew 28:16-20

Teacher's Notes

The *Teacher's Notes* are optional but provide a space for you to document which Bible verse you choose and any other discussion points, songs, verses or notes you wish to keep record of for your student.

SARAH, PLAIN AND TALL

Date:

Student:

Five in a Row Bible Verse(s):

_____
_____
_____
_____
_____
_____
_____
_____

☐ Memorized Verse(s) / Copywork

Character Trait or Life Lesson to apply:

_____
_____
_____

Related Worship Songs/Hymns

_____
_____
_____
_____
_____

Misc. Notes:

_____
_____
_____
_____
_____
_____
_____
_____
_____
_____

Have your student draw a picture or write a reflection on the Bible verse(s) in the space below.

Homer Price

Chapter 1—The Case of the Sensational Scent

Centerburg must have been shocked! Imagine—four masked men stealing Mr. Blott's prize money. Why would they steal? The Bible talks about **stealing** and how it is against God's principles. In fact, God even made a list of His ways called the Ten Commandments. Share with your student God's eighth commandment, which says "You shall not steal" (Exodus 20:15).

Exodus 20:15

Stealing hurts the person we're stealing from, but it also hurts us. By breaking one of God's laws, we are damaging our own soul. When we sin, it causes a rift between God and us. Because of God's love, with confession and forgiveness, that rift can be healed. But it is always better to obey God in the first place than to have to seek His forgiveness, after the fact. Discuss with your student the sad state of someone who would steal. But don't forget to remind your student of God's forgiveness for those who do and who repent of their sin.

Chapter 2—The Case of the Cosmic Comic

Homer and Freddy were excited to see the real Super Duper! They were sure he would exhibit his amazing strength or death-defying bravery. When the boys saw the Super Duper unable to save himself from a minor car wreck, they were disappointed. Discuss human limitations with your student. Just like the man who pretended to be the real Super Duper, no human is invincible. No human can live forever. Human beings, even our own parents and other people we deeply respect, can let us down sometimes. We all have faults, so no human can be perfect. But God is!

Our Heavenly Father is the only one we can put all our **trust and hope** in. He will never let us down. He will never leave us or forsake us and He can defeat and conquer any evil (unlike the Super Duper).

In Romans 5:5, the Word tells us that if we have hope in God, He will not disappoint us. He fills our hearts with love and joy and is always with us to help guide and protect. Hebrews 10:22-23 tells us God is always faithful to his children!

Romans 5:5

Hebrews 10:22-23

Five in a Row Bible Supplement

Romans 8:24
Romans 15:13
1 Timothy 5:5
Titus 2:13
Hebrews 11:1

Share with your student more verses dealing with hope, and remind her that God will always meet and exceed our expectations: Romans 8:24, 15:13, 1 Timothy 5:5, Titus 2:13, Hebrews 11:1.

Chapter 3—The Doughnuts

Why did the people buy so many doughnuts? There was a reward of great value being offered! Instead of just eating doughnuts, suddenly people were looking for that very expensive diamond bracelet! When something is worth a lot and it is lost, we will look for it diligently.

Matthew 13:45
Matthew 13:44

The Bible talks about both us searching for God and God searching for us. In Matthew 13:45, Jesus compared the kingdom of God to a rare pearl—a jewel like the rich lady's bracelet. Share with your student the parable Jesus tells about the man who, upon finding the pearl of great price, sold all that he had to buy the field in which it was found (Matthew 13:44). That's commitment!

Just like that man, we should be searching with all our heart for the kingdom of God. And when we find that **treasure**, we should value it above all else.

Matthew 18:10-13

Likewise, the Bible speaks of God's great love for us. When we're lost, He looks for us! Isn't that glorious! In Matthew 18:10-13, Jesus tells the story of the shepherd with 100 sheep. Ninety-nine of the sheep stay with him but one wanders off. That shepherd leaves the 99 and searches diligently until he finds the one lost lamb. Just like that shepherd, our Heavenly Father does not want anyone to be lost. And He will search for us until He finds us!

Chapter 4—Mystery Yarn

Miss Terwilliger is a very thrifty woman! She doesn't seem to worry much about what the future holds. She knows she has enough for now and will make do with what she has later. The Bible includes many verses about **trusting God** to care for us. Our Heavenly Father doesn't want us to worry about our own needs, but instead wants us to spend our time helping others. In Luke 12:27, Jesus compares us to the lilies—beautiful and lovely just as we are!

Luke 12:27

The Lord cares for each sparrow in the world. Just imagine how much more He cares for His own children! The Bible tells us if we look to the Lord first and seek His Kingdom, all our needs will be met. The Lord's priorities may seem backwards to us, but His ways are often like that. If we seek Him, He will care for us. If we promote others to places of honor, we will be honored ourselves. Remind your student to rest in the Lord and delight in Him. It is in this way that we gain the desires of our hearts (Psalm 37:4) and all the things we need are added unto us. The Lord does not forget His own!

Psalm 37:4

Chapter 5—Nothing New Under the Sun (Hardly)

Mr. Murphy is new to Centerburg. He has no friends and no one even knows his real name. Homer makes friends with Mr. Murphy and finally finds out what is under the big canvas on the back of his truck. The Bible talks about being **kind to strangers**. Share with your student the following stories and verses in the Bible.

Draw your student's attention to Hebrews 13:2, where the Bible tells us to care for and entertain strangers. The Word tells us that some people have taken care of angels without even knowing it, just thinking they were strangers. Imagine that—what an honor! And yet the Bible tells us to treat all strangers with kindness and respect because we can never tell who they are.

Hebrews 13:2

Take some time out to read these two wonderful, heart-warming books with similar themes: *Papa Panov's Special Day* by Ruben Saillens and *Always Room for One More* by Sorche Nic Leodhas. *Papa Panov* is based on an old French tale and was adapted by Leo Tolstoy. *Always Room* is based on a Scottish folk song. Both storybooks have fabulous writing, incredible illustrations (*Always Room* won the Caldecott Medal) and touch the spiritual issues of caring for strangers in a sweet and gentle way.

Another example of caring for strangers is the parable of the Good Samaritan. In this tale, found in Luke 10:25-37, Jesus tells the story of a Jewish man who is robbed, beaten and left for dead in the street. Later on in the day a priest stops, looks at the man and passes by. A while later, a Levite comes to the man in the

Luke 10:25-37

Five in a Row Bible Supplement

road, and passes by. Finally, a Samaritan, from a group considered morally and religiously bankrupt, stops and bandages the stranger's wounds, loads him onto his donkey, takes him to town and pays for his keep in an area inn before leaving.

The moral of our story? Jesus tells us to be merciful, just like the Samaritan. We should care for strangers we see (even if it's a person we wouldn't normally seek as a friend).

Encourage your student to be kind to new people and to remember the story of the Good Samaritan!

Chapter 6—Wheels of Progress

Miss Enders is a **generous** woman! The Bible emphasizes the importance of giving. Being generous comes from the heart of a good and kind person. The Lord desires that we all display these characteristics in our lives.

Galatians 5:22-23

Philippians 1:6

Goodness and kindness are included in a special list of godly characteristics called the fruit of the Spirit. Look with your student at the passage in Galatians 5:22-23. What are the other "fruits?" It should always be our desire to acquire and practice these positive traits in our life. Sometimes we fail and act in ways that go against God's principles; we act selfishly or out of spite. But remember, He who is faithful will continue the good work He has begun in us (Philippians 1:6). Despite our own failures, God is willing to soften our hearts and help us grow in the fruit of the Spirit. Never be discouraged. Just be willing to try again!

# Teacher's Notes

The *Teacher's Notes* are optional but provide a space for you to document which Bible verse you choose and any other discussion points, songs, verses or notes you wish to keep record of for your student.

HOMER PRICE

Date:

Student:

Five in a Row Bible Verse(s):

_____
_____
_____
_____
_____
_____
_____
_____

☐ Memorized Verse(s) / Copywork

Character Trait or Life Lesson to apply:

_____
_____
_____

Related Worship Songs/Hymns

_____
_____
_____
_____
_____

Misc. Notes:

_____
_____
_____
_____
_____
_____
_____
_____
_____
_____

Have your student draw a picture or write a reflection on the Bible verse(s) in the space below.

Five in a Row Bible Supplement

The Saturdays

Chapter 1—Saturday One

In this chapter we read, "All the Melendy children had their own jobs. They each had not one but several.... And the cleaning had to be thorough." The Melendy children work happily at their jobs around the house. They don't love the work, but they don't complain. They understand that **working** is a part of life, and the quicker and more cheerfully it is accomplished, the better.

Colossians 3:23

The Bible tells us that whatever the Lord gives us to do, we should do it with our whole heart. Even if our job is to make the bed each morning and take out the garbage once a week, it's important to do that job just as if we were doing it for Jesus (Colossians 3:23). This makes sense, doesn't it? By honoring our parents and doing our chores with happy hearts, we are really honoring the Lord.

Chapter 2—Saturday Two

Mrs. Oliphant disobeys her father when she runs away to the carnival. He expressly forbids her to attend the event, but she does it anyway. In the end, Mrs. Oliphant was blessed to return home safely. But along the way, many terrible things happened to her and she was treated badly by Zenaida and Bastien. Her life could have been spared a lot of grief if only she had obeyed her father.

Sometimes when parents don't allow children to do things, it doesn't seem to make any sense. Children can't see the problems or dangers that adults sometimes see. They may feel frustration and anger because they aren't allowed to do certain things.

Exodus 20:12

Unlike Mrs. Oliphant, however, God asks us to **honor** our father and mother and **obey** their requests. In Exodus 20:12, the Bible tells us to honor our parents because it is pleasing to the Lord. Even when we don't understand and think our plans are better, we must put God's will before that and obey His laws. For our safety, God has given parents special wisdom and experience. Talk with your student about why God asks children to obey their parents—that it will keep them safe and happy, and will bring delight to their Heavenly Father. You could discuss how children can tell parents about their frustrations and questions, but in the end, let parents have the final say. You may want to look over more verses in the Bible on this topic, including Proverbs 10:1, 17:21, 23:22 and 24, 29:3, Matthew 15:4 and Ephesians 6:2.

Chapter 3—Saturday Three

Rush goes to the opera house and listens to wonderful **music**. Each player in the orchestra is a gifted musician who plays his instrument wonderfully. The Bible talks about beautiful music as well. In Ephesians 5:19, the Bible tells us to give thanks to the Lord, singing songs and making music in our hearts for him. David, a famous king in the Bible, was also a musician and composer. Many of the lovely psalms are actually songs David wrote and sang to the Lord. In Psalm 27, for example, David sings about seeking the Lord on high and having confidence in His strength.

Our Heavenly Father loves each and every thing about us. He created us—from our noses to our little fingers. Hearing us sing songs and lift our voices to Him brings Him pleasure. It doesn't matter if our voices aren't the best, or if we don't know how to play an instrument. Whatever we can bring Him in song will be beautiful to His ears. He loves each of us! Here are more verses about music and song: Judges 5:3, Psalms 95:2, 98:4, and 108:1.

Chaper 4—Saturday Four

While it was being done, Mona certainly had fun getting her hair done and nails painted, didn't she? Even though she knew her father wouldn't approve, she thought it would be all right. Mona tried to rationalize her choice. After all, her father hadn't actually said, "Mona, you may not get your hair cut, nails done, etc." But in her heart, she knew exctly what her father would say if she asked him. Later, after she showed everyone what she had done, Mona wished she had never decided to go to the beauty shop.

Sin and disobedience can be fun in the moment, but it is later that we pay for our mistake. Sometimes we think that sin is only an unhappy, painful thing. If that were true, overcoming temptation would be easy! Who would want to do

---

Proverbs 10:1
Proverbs 17:21
Proverbs 23:22 & 24
Proverbs 29:3
Matthew 15:4
Ephesians 6:2

Ephesians 5:19

Psalm 27

Judges 5:3
Psalm 95:2
Psalm 98:4
Psalm 108:1

something that would only cause pain? Unfortunately, doing what we know is wrong can hold great appeal and delight a lot of the time. This is why it is difficult to listen to God's Word and choose what is right. Sin can be a lot of fun at first, but later we will be sorry that we chose unwisely.

1 John 3:6
Exodus 20:20
Proverbs 23:17
Romans 5:8

Discuss with your student that when she is tempted like Mona, to remember how sad Mona was later. She can decide in her heart to do what will please the Lord and her parents—to do what she knows is right! Here are some verses about sin you can share with your student: 1 John 3:6, Exodus 20:20, Proverbs 23:17 and Romans 5:8.

Chapter 5—Saturday Five

Oliver is **lost and frightened** when he leaves the circus. He doesn't know the way home and he feels a little ill. Discuss with your student times when you've both had this experience, or when you've had times of fear and loneliness. Remember that we can always turn to God. He is ready to help and listen to our fears anytime. It doesn't matter where we are, how alone we feel, or who is around us—we can always call and pray to the One who loves us more than anything. He is waiting for us to talk to Him and He will comfort and guide us (Psalm 23:4). Does your student think she should only pray to God when she has a serious problem? Remind her that even if she is just feeling frustrated, God is ready to listen to her and comfort her.

Psalm 23:4

Chapter 6—Saturday Six

The Melendy children and Cuffy could have been seriously hurt during the coal gas scare. Instead, they were blessed to be alerted and solve the situation promptly. God is our ultimate **protector**. The angels He directs watch over us and care for us. When frightening situations like the coal gas happen, God is protecting us even then.

Psalm 32:7
Psalm 17:8

In Psalm 32:7 we read that God will protect us from trouble. He will shield us with His wings (Psalm 17:8). Remind your student that she can rest in the knowledge of God's protection and thank Him for His faithfulness.

Chapter 7—Saturday Seven

Imagine how refreshing that ice cream was to the Melendy children. After spending steamy summer days penned up in the house, Mrs. Oliphant offers them a true treat!

The Lord understands all our needs. He understands that sometimes life gets a little stressful or difficult, and what we need is **refreshment**—a comforting, peaceful time. Just as He supplies our other needs, the Lord also is a source of renewal for our spirits (Psalm 103:5, Isaiah 40:31). Like a cool drink of water, Jesus longs to bring good things to us every day: a cool breeze, a funny little rabbit, even a simple flower are God's ways of saying, "Hey, I love you! Relax!" Mention to your student that she can remember to look for God's "refreshments" every day.

Psalm 103:5
Isaiah 40:31

Chapter 8—Saturday Eight

The Melendys are a **strong, happy family**, aren't they? The children are kind and good to one another. They love and respect their father and Cuffy. They do good deeds for others and uphold good values. They make mistakes, but they try their best.

God longs for families to be close and strong, just like the Melendy family. He understands the best thing children can do to help this happen is to honor their parents (Exodus 20:12). Discuss with your student practical ways she can show love to others, including her parents. Ideas might include saying please and thank you, helping around the house, and generally being pleasant to live with. Life is much richer when you have a strong family. With your student, determine to do your part to achieve this goal and honor the Lord each day! He will smile!

Exodus 20:12

Five in a Row Bible Supplement

Teacher's Notes

The *Teacher's Notes* are optional but provide a space for you to document which Bible verse you choose and any other discussion points, songs, verses or notes you wish to keep record of for your student.

THE SATURDAYS

Date:

Student:

Five in a Row **Bible Verse(s):**

☐ Memorized Verse(s) / Copywork

Character Trait or Life Lesson to apply:

Related Worship Songs/Hymns

Misc. Notes:

Have your student draw a picture or write a reflection on the Bible verse(s) in the space below.

The Saturdays

Helen Keller

Chapter 1

Helen Keller is blind. She will never see a sunset, or watch her mother's face or notice when her father is smiling. How sad! When Jesus was here on earth, He performed miracles and healed people of many kinds of illnesses. Share with your student the story of **blind Bartimaeus** and his healing found in Mark 10:46-52. One day, Jesus and His disciples were walking through Jericho. Suddenly a man came out of the crowd and began shouting to Jesus, "Have mercy on me, Son of David!" Jesus stopped and talked with the man. He asked Bartimaeus what he wanted Him to do for him. Bartimaeus says, "I want to see." And because of his faith in God, Jesus told him he was healed. And Bartimaeus was! He could immediately see and rejoiced. Then he began to follow Jesus and the disciples. Can you imagine being there and watching such an awesome miracle? The Lord is good.

Mark 10:46-52

Chapter 2

Helen could not see or hear anything. What difficult challenges to overcome! Learning to be **thankful** for everything is an important part of living gracious, godly lives. Does your student ever get bored reading school assignments? What if you couldn't read at all? Walking, talking, running, singing, holding a pencil, reading, doing a cartwheel—being thankful for everything is our way of responding to God's goodness in our lives. In the Bible, the Lord tells us to be thankful in all things (1 Thessalonians 5:18). And when you see someone who is less fortunate than yourself, pray for her and remind yourself to say "thank you" to Jesus once again for your blessings. We are so blessed—be thankful today! (2 Corinthians 2:14, Psalm 100:4)

1 Thessalonians 5:18

2 Corinthians 2:14
Psalm 100:4

Chapter 3

Mrs. Keller wanted to simply give in and let Helen have the doll back. But Miss Annie said that Helen needs to learn self-control and discipline. If Miss Annie wants Helen to be happy, shouldn't she let her have the doll? Not necessarily. Just because things are painful, does not always mean they are bad for us. Sometimes when the Lord wants to teach us lessons, He **disciplines** us. It isn't always fun, but it helps us

Five in a Row Bible Supplement

grow and causes our hearts to be more like His. In the end, His discipline shows us how much He loves us. The Bible says something about that in Proverbs 3:12, Hebrews 12:6, and 12:10. Read these passages with your student today and remember—when we think we're being disciplined, we're also being loved!

Proverbs 3:12
Hebrews 12:6
Hebrews 12:10

Chapter 4

Helen doesn't have much **self-control**. She runs from activity to activity and hits people when she is angry. Is this her fault? Probably not. She doesn't understand how to communicate with others so she struggles—because she doesn't understand. But Miss Annie knows she must teach her student to control herself, if Helen is ever going to succeed in her relationships with other people.

Galatians 5:22-23

The Bible talks a great deal about the importance of self-control. Our Heavenly Father even lists it as one of the fruits of the Spirit (Galatians 5:22-23)—the important character traits we should see developing in our life. When we practice self-control, we allow ourselves to think beyond our immediate wants and desires. We begin to act more like Jesus. Read with your student the following Scriptures about self-control and pray together today that the Lord would begin a greater work of self-control within you! (2 Peter 1:5-7, Titus 2:11-12)

2 Peter 1:5-7
Titus 2:11-12

Chapters 5-6

John 20:24-31

Helen begins to learn all about the world through Teacher's hands and fingers. As Teacher spells words into Helen's hands, the young girl begins to make connections and learn the truth about the world around her. Share with your student the Biblical passage found in John 20:24-31. After Jesus' crucifixion and resurrection, He reappeared to His disciples. But one disciple, Thomas, did not believe it was Him. Even as Jesus stood before him, **Thomas still doubted**. It wasn't until the Lord Jesus displayed His hands to Thomas and the doubtful disciple saw the nail marks, that he believed. Jesus then tells Thomas how blessed he is to have seen and believed. He also blesses all of us, who have not seen Jesus in the flesh, but still believe in Him!

Chapter 7

Helen receives many gifts for Christmas. She can't even walk across the floor without stepping on tissue paper. And the days before Helen's holiday were filled with cookie baking and tree decorating. **Christmas** is a beautiful holiday filled with traditions and family memories. Certainly gift-giving, stockings and evergreen trees are some of the best parts. But what is the most important part of Christmas? What is the reason for the holiday? The birth of our Lord Jesus Christ. Take a few moments to remember the true meaning of this special day. Reread the story of Mary, Joseph and Jesus found in Luke 2. Spend some time meditating on the miracle of Christ's birth and how blessed we are to have such a loving and caring Heavenly Father. Merry Christmas and blessed be the name of the Lord!

Luke 2

Chapter 8

Helen spoke her first sentence, but her speech was growly and slurred. Although Helen would try all of her life, she would never learn to speak completely clearly. But, despite this handicap and her blindness and deafness, Helen Keller lived a life of purpose and strength. She inspired generations of people. Helen didn't let her weaknesses stop her from doing the things she felt called to do.

Does your student know that Moses, the man who led the Israelites out of bondage and across the Red Sea, had speech difficulties? When the Lord asked him to lead His people out of slavery, Moses told Him he couldn't. In Exodus 4:10-17, Moses said, "I'm not good at speaking to people. I'm not eloquent and I'm slow." The Lord encouraged Moses and told him that He would give him the words. But still, Moses pleaded for the Lord to find someone else. Finally, the Lord provided Moses with a helper—his brother Aaron. The Lord told Moses to tell Aaron what to say, and he would be the voice. In this way, Moses did not need to be insecure. He had someone to help him. Whenever you feel like you are inadequate, remember that our Lord is a powerful and loving Lord. He wants to see you succeed! And He looks for **opportunities to help us** and give us the strength to complete what has been asked of us. If you feel insecure or weak, run to the Lord and tell Him. He will meet you in that place and help you rise above your pain.

Exodus 4:10-17

Five in a Row Bible Supplement

Chapter 9

Helen not only graduated from prestigious Radcliffe College, but she graduated with honors! It had been a long and difficult road, but Helen Keller had completed her goal. She was a college graduate. In each person's life, there will be challenges to overcome. The Lord's will for our lives is that we do our best and **persevere** to glorify God. Read 1 Corinthians 9:24, 2 Timothy 4:7 and Hebrews 12:1 with your student. Encourage him to strive for the highest goal in everything he does. God has plans for our lives, and we don't know all that they contain. But if we give it our all, we will be successful—and a blessing to God and others!

1 Corinthians 9:24
2 Timothy 4:7
Hebrews 12:1

Chapter 10

On page 82 we read, "Helen knew that many [blind and deaf people] led lonely lives with no families and few friends. Often they were too poor to go to school. Helen was determined to do something useful."

Helen Keller gave of herself for most of her life, devoting her energies to improving the life of blind and deaf people. She had received so much, she felt she should give back. What does the Bible say about such **selfless giving**? We read that when the Lord called Abram (Genesis 12:2-3), He said to him, "I will bless you ... so that you will be a blessing." When God gives us great gifts of talents, wisdom or even forgiveness, He expects us to give those things back to others. In the New Testament (Matthew 10:8), Jesus tells us, "You received without paying; give without pay." If we hold in the good things God has given us, then they can never be of service to others. If you feel blessed today, then turn and share that blessing with someone else. In this way, you are giving of yourself and pleasing the heart of God!

Genesis 12:2-3

Matthew 10:8

Teacher's Notes

The *Teacher's Notes* are optional but provide a space for you to document which Bible verse you choose and any other discussion points, songs, verses or notes you wish to keep record of for your student.

HELEN KELLER

Date:

Student:

Five in a Row Bible Verse(s):

☐ Memorized Verse(s) / Copywork

Character Trait or Life Lesson to apply:

Related Worship Songs/Hymns

Misc. Notes:

Have your student draw a picture or write a reflection on the Bible verse(s) in the space below.

Five in a Row Bible Supplement

Skylark

Chapter 1

Caleb and Anna understand that Sarah's name is not written in the land. What do we mean when we talk about having a name "written in the land?" One way to describe it is that the land is important to us—we value it and respect it. The Bible talks about having the Lord's precepts and wisdom written, not on the land, but on our hearts! Our Father's desire is for us to love, serve and obey Him. He wants us to remember His laws and value them. Share Proverbs 7:3 and Hebrews 8:10 with your student and talk about how we can have our Heavenly Father's name "written on our heart." By reading the Word of God each day, going to church, and praying for guidance in our relationships with friends and family, we are **"writing" on our hearts** the very heart of our Father!

Proverbs 7:3
Hebrews 8:10

Chapter 2

"You fell in love with us." Caleb knows he is loved by Sarah. He is not afraid to say it. Anna and Caleb both know how much Sarah and Papa adore them. Do you know the Lord is in love with us? That He delights in watching over us? In His Word (Psalm 25:10, 147:11, Revelation 1:5), God tells us how much **He loves us** and wants to see us succeed. As much as we love Jesus, we cannot even comprehend the depth of His delight in us. We can say to our Heavenly Father, just as Caleb did, "You fell in love with us!"

Psalm 25:10
Psalm 147:11
Revelation 1:5

Chapter 3

Mame has her new calf, Moonbeam, in the barn—a natural place for a calf to be born. Has your student ever been in a barn or horse stable? Even with clean straw and bedding, it's still fairly dirty and not a fit place for people to sleep. What about a newborn baby? Can you imagine an infant in a stable box? But, in fact, that is just what happened to Jesus when He was born.

Luke 2:1-7

Share with your student the amazing story of **Jesus' birth**. Found in Luke 2:1-7, we see His young parents, Mary and Joseph, unable to find a room for the night. They have been traveling and Mary is nearly ready to have her baby. Imagine how uncomfortable she was, riding on the back of a donkey all day long, with no prospect of a hotel room.

Finally, an innkeeper, unable to rent them a room because he was already booked, offers them the stable—the barn with the cows and horses! Grateful for somewhere to stay, Mary and Joseph accepted, and it was there that Jesus was born. Instead of a nice cradle, carved by His carpenter father, baby Jesus was laid, wrapped in strips of cloth, in a manger—a cattle trough filled with hay.

Just like Moonbeam, our Savior and Messiah was born in a stable. The Bible tells us that the Father sometimes hides things from wise people, and reveals Himself to the littlest of children (Matthew 11:25). Who, of the wise rulers and kings of Jesus' time, would have believed that the Messiah had been born in a stable? It takes faith to believe when circumstances do not make sense. Jesus was sent to Earth to save all people—rich and poor alike. The significance of His humble beginning only serves to illustrate this truth all the more. What a wonderful Savior we serve!

Matthew 11:25

Chapter 4

Caleb demonstrates great hope by placing his glass outside for the rain. The Bible shares many insights about **hope**. When outside circumstances beyond our control arise, we can rest in the assurance that the Lord will always supply our needs. We can place our hope in God and His perfect plan for our lives. Share with your student some of the following verses regarding hope, and be encouraged today: Psalms 39:7, 43:5, 71:5, 71:14, Jeremiah 14:8, and Ezra 10:2. Psalm 71:5 says that the Lord has been the psalmist's hope, even from his youth. Will you be able to say this too?

Psalm 39:7
Psalm 43:5
Psalm 71:5
Psalm 71:14
Jeremiah 14:8
Ezra 10:2

Chapter 5

The Wittings would have been very grateful for some water. As their well level drops lower and lower, the water becomes more and more valuable. What are the things you are **thankful** for? Sometimes, because we are so blessed, we forget to say "thank you" to the Lord for the little things. Our health, breathing each day, our family, even water! The Bible tells us to give thanks in all things (1 Thessalonians 5:18). But what about when something is going wrong? When we're frustrated and sad? Yes, even then we can find things to be thankful for—

1 Thessalonians 5:18

Five in a Row Bible Supplement

even something as simple as water. Learning to be grateful and to notice the small things in life is important both in our relationships with others and in our relationship with our Heavenly Father. He is a good Father, who provides all our needs. Remember to say "thank you" to Him today!

Chapter 6

Fire is an amazing thing to watch, but it can also be destructive. Papa and Sarah had to fight the flames in their field. If they had not been able to stop it, the fire could have burned their home down! Fire consumes what it touches. However, there is a wonderful story in the Bible about a bush that caught on fire and was not burned at all. Imagine how amazed you'd be if you saw such a thing!

Exodus 3:1-10

Share with your student this wonderful tale found in Exodus 3:1-10. In the story, we see Moses approached by God on his way through the desert. Moses is busily tending his father-in-law's flock of sheep, when suddenly he sees flames of fire come up from within a bush. Moses quickly assesses the situation. The bush is on fire, but it is not being burned at all! Then, when he goes closer to inspect the amazing sight, the Lord speaks to him and tells Moses the mission He has for him. It was in this awesome and supernatural way that Moses found out he had been chosen to lead the Israelites out of slavery in Egypt. It is also in this passage that we learn one of God's many names—I Am. Fire usually consumes what it touches, but not in Moses' case!

Chapter 7

Maggie and Matthew must move from their home on the prairie because they have no water. They think if they don't move, things could only get worse. Can you imagine being faced with starvation from famine? Or death from drought? What a frightening situation.

1 Kings 17:7-16

In the Bible, we see many accounts where the Lord saves people from situations just like that. One wonderful story is found in 1 Kings 17:7-16. In this tale we find Elijah the prophet in a town called Zarephath. Zarephath was experiencing a terrible **drought**, even worse than the one the Wittings are dealing with. Because of the drought, there was also widespread famine in the land. No one had any food. Elijah is told by the Lord to find and visit a certain widow and her son. When he goes to her and asks her for some bread she says she has only enough flour to make one more meal for her and her son. Then they will most certainly die. Elijah, under the instruction of the Lord, tells her to fix him some bread and them some for herself. She obeys and for the rest of the famine, her pot is never empty of flour! Every day she finds the same amount still in the jar—enough for food each day. Isn't it miraculous what God can accomplish? He takes care of His children—He knows our every need.

Chapter 8

Despite the drought, everyone cheers up when Sarah's birthday arrives. Not only is it a happy occasion, but her aunts have sent her a phonograph. The **music** makes their hearts light. Does your student know that the book of Psalms is really a book of songs? Many of them, David (the King of Israel) wrote when he was a young shepherd. They are songs to the Lord. What does your student think the music might have sounded like which accompanied them? Read the following psalms: Psalm 8, Psalm 11 or your personal favorites. Draw your student's attention to the text located underneath the chapter heading. "For the choirmaster. Of David." Some of the psalms are happy, joyful songs, and some were written when David was sad and frustrated. Just like Sarah, however, the music must have helped lift his spirits. God is the giver of all good things (James 1:17). Aren't you thankful He thought of music?

Psalm 8
Psalm 11

James 1:17

Chapter 9

When the Wittings' barn was on fire, it must have been a terrible, but awesome, sight. Imagine how high the flames must have reached—if they had neighbors nearby, then surely everyone would have noticed. Fire is a frightening thing to see, but it also fascinates us, doesn't it? Does your student know that the Lord Himself was present in a **pillar of fire** once? In Exodus 13:20-22, the Bible tells us that the Lord led the Israelites through the desert. He was always ahead of them. In the day, His Spirit was present in a pillar of cloud. And at night, He led them in a pillar of fire! They couldn't really "see" God, but they knew He was

Exodus 13:20-22

there. His glory and presence were all around them and He wanted them to know He was there. The Bible tells us that neither the cloud during the day, nor the fire at night ever left the Israelites. Even when we think God has forsaken us and we cannot see Him, He will always be there.

Chapter 10

Aunt Mattie, Aunt Harriet and Aunt Lou are very welcoming, aren't they? They kiss Sarah, Anna and Caleb and offer them food and drinks. It must have been easy to love Anna and Caleb—they are so wonderful. But what happens when you meet someone you don't particularly like right away? What if they are mean to you? Being **kind to others** is an important part of being a Christian. The Bible says that just as Jesus loves us, we are to love others (John 13:34). Even when things aren't going just the way we want them to, we should always strive to show others respect and kindness. This is what Jesus did for us. We cannot show less to others.

John 13:34

Chapter 11

Papa's letter to Anna shows how much he misses his daughter—and Caleb and Sarah. They've been apart for a long while. Draw your student's attention to the following verses (written by the Apostle Paul) in the letters to the Romans and others: Romans 1:1 and 7, 1 Corinthians 16:7, Ephesians 1:1 and 15 and Philippians 1:1-3. Remind your student that the New Testament books which Paul wrote, were **letters** to his friends in other regions. He wrote down what the Lord had been telling him, and also included personal notes and prayers. Just like Papa, Paul told his friends what he missed about them and how he was thinking of them. When we look at these books in that personal light, we begin to understand them better. We can read books like 1 Corinthians and Romans remembering that they are letters to us from God!

Romans 1:1 & 7
1 Corinthians 16:7
Ephesians 1:1 & 15
Philippians 1:1-3

Chapter 12

Aunt Lou went skinny-dipping in the moonlight. That was probably a funny sight—at least Caleb thought so. Sometimes, however, just because something is funny doesn't mean it is the best thing to do in any given time or place. **Modesty** is important to God. Share 1 Timothy 2:9-10 with your student. As Christians, the way we dress, speak and act reflects on our faith. Dressing appropriately and speaking kindly are two things we must think about. Discuss with your student what he thinks of this verse and topic. Share some of your thoughts. Modesty is a subjective topic, and different families and individuals are likely to have different points of view, but it's a topic that all Christians should carefully consider and pray about.

1 Timothy 2:9-10

Chapters 13-15

Caleb misses Papa very much. He goes off to be alone. When Anna finds him, he's crying. Anna comforts him, but sometimes people just can't take **sadness** away. Has your student ever had a hurt or fear that just didn't seem to subside, no matter how much he was comforted? We have a loving, gentle Heavenly Father who wants to comfort us. Unlike people, the Lord can always provide healing and peace. In Psalm 70, David writes in his song that the Lord is his help and deliverer. If you ever feel worried about something, or hurt and don't know who to turn to, ask Jesus to bring you peace and joy. He promises He will.

Psalm 70

Teacher's Notes

The *Teacher's Notes* are optional but provide a space for you to document which Bible verse you choose and any other discussion points, songs, verses or notes you wish to keep record of for your student.

SKYLARK

Date:

Student:

Five in a Row **Bible Verse(s):**

☐ Memorized Verse(s) / Copywork

Character Trait or Life Lesson to apply:

Related Worship Songs/Hymns

Misc. Notes:

Have your student draw a picture or write a reflection on the Bible verse(s) in the space below.

The Story of George Washington Carver

Chapter 1

Moses Carver told people he did not agree with slavery. He said he thought it was wrong, but he owned slaves anyway. What happens when we **say one thing and do another**? Why do we sometimes say what we know is right and then do the wrong thing? The Bible talks about this very issue in 2 Peter 2:21. The Lord tells us that it would be better for us to not even know what is right, than to say we do and then ignore our hearts. It isn't enough to talk about doing the right thing. Talking is easy. It's the doing that is tough. Learning to submit your own will and obey what the Lord asks of you is the important part. We don't know what Moses Carver truly believed was right in his own heart, but we can look at his actions. Remember to listen to the Lord and obey what your conscience is telling you.

2 Peter 2:21

Chapter 2

George is only seven years old, but he has learned a lot about plants. Even adults come to him for his advice and answers. People recognize his **wisdom**. Does your student know Jesus was very young when He began to talk with the adults in His community? The Bible tells us (Luke 2:41-49) that one day His mother and father couldn't find Him. They asked His friends and their relatives. Nobody could tell them where Jesus was. Finally, after three whole days, they found Him sitting in the temple in Jerusalem. Jesus was just sitting there, among the great teachers, talking with them about the Scriptures and asking and answering questions. He was only twelve years old! The Bible tells us that Jesus grew in wisdom and stature and in favor with God and men (Luke 2:52). God loves children and He desires to use them and to give them purpose—just as much as adults. Don't let yourself become discouraged if you are young and don't think God can use you. God will use anyone who has a heart for Him!

Luke 2:41-49

Luke 2:52

Chapter 3

George and his brother, Jim, are very different. George is not as strong or healthy as Jim, but both boys help Uncle Moses and Aunt Susan in the ways they are able. Remind your student of another set of very different brothers—Jacob and

Five in a Row Bible Supplement

Genesis 25:21-27

Esau. Read the account found in Genesis 25:21-27. Isaac and Rebekah pray to the Lord for children and the Lord grants their request. Rebekah is soon pregnant with twin sons! When the baby boys arrive, they name the firstborn Esau, and the secondborn Jacob. Esau, like Jim Carver, was big for his age and strong. He enjoyed hunting and hiking through the country. Jacob, more like George, was small and preferred to stay in the tents with the women. Jacob grew very close to his mother, Rebekah. Encourage your student to remember that **all children are different**—but each is made in God's image and loved by Him dearly!

Chapter 4

Even though George wasn't sure he could go inside, he **went to church** every Sunday and sat on the steps outside. Singing hymns, listening to the sermon, and observing the Lord's day was important to George. In the Bible (Exodus 20:8), one of the Ten Commandments states: "Remember the Sabbath day, to keep it holy." For many people, attending a church, parish or temple service is a vital part of that commandment. Honoring God every day in our speech, activities and relationships is important—and so is remembering to honor Him on the Sabbath. By giving the glory to God in our hearts each week at a special time, we are honoring Him all the time. George understood the importance of attending services regularly—let him serve as a reminder for all of us! It pleases the heart of God when we follow His commandments and respect His requests.

Exodus 20:8

Chapter 5

When George arrives in Neosho, he doesn't know a single person. He is hungry and tired. He is almost ready to head back home, when he meets up with Aunt Mariah. The Lord provided a wonderful place for George. The Watkins feed him, give him a home and treat him as their own son. What are some of the things the Lord has done for you in hard times? Share with your student the story of the **Israelites and the manna**, found in Exodus 16. Here we find the Israelites, led by Moses and Aaron, fleeing Egypt and their slavery. The Lord made a way for them to escape, but after a few months of wandering, they are tired and hungry. They begin to grumble and complain. Once again, out of His

Exodus 16

mercy, the Lord does not get angry but instead makes a wonderful provision for His people. He sends them a special food called manna from the sky each day. Manna was small flakes that tasted like bread and honey. The Israelites were able to gather manna each day and provide food for each family. Each day the Lord supplies our needs—sometimes in miraculous ways. What special provisions has the Lord made in your life? Share your stories and thank the Lord together for His abundant gifts to all of us!

Chapter 6

In this chapter we read about the horrific treatment of a black man in Fort Scott and George's reaction. We also read that George knew hate was a sin. Certainly the mob of white men beating and killing the black man in our story was a vicious crime and grieved the Lord. But what if the mob of angry people hadn't actually injured the man, but simply hated him in their hearts? Would that be a sin? When we think a hateful thought, do we still grieve the heart of our Father? Yes. The Bible teaches us to fend off thoughts of hate and anger, and instead to act in love and peace. Read with your student Leviticus 19:17, where the Lord tells His people not to hate their brothers, but instead to love them as they love themselves. In Luke 6:27-31, Jesus tells us to love our enemies—to pray for them —to bless them. Often when we are being mistreated or hurt, our first reaction is to become angry and hateful. But we must learn to act in love, reflecting the heart of our Father to others! Pray for each other today and ask for greater grace in loving your enemies.

Leviticus 19:17

Luke 6:27-31

Chapter 7

The Seymours and George moved to Minneapolis, Kansas. They went by train. Draw your student's attention to the sentence that reads: "Even though George was over sixteen, he was so small that he only had to buy a child's ticket." What does your student think of this action? If George looked younger than he was, was it right for the Seymours not to tell the station master his real age? Is that a major issue or just a minor infraction?

Five in a Row Bible Supplement

Luke 19:17 — Share with your student the passage found in Luke 19:17. The Lord tells us if we are **faithful in the smallest things**, He will give us more. Just because it was a simple train fare and no one would ever know, doesn't make it right. The Lord sees our hearts and our actions. Encourage your student to be faithful in the little, so he will be granted much.

Chapter 8

Poor George arrives at college, only to be rejected because he is black. The author tells us that "George felt tears come into his eyes." Have you ever **cried** when hurt, misunderstood or disappointed? The Bible tells us that each tear we shed is precious to God. He knows when we're hurting and understands when we've been hurt or misjudged. Psalm 56:8 tells us that He remembers all of our sadness and pain. Share this important concept with your student. It doesn't take away our hurts, but it at least reminds us that God understands, cares and shares them with us. A person's worth is encompassed in the fact that God has made him and loves him. Knowing that God cares and works all things together for our good (Romans 8:28) can help take the sting away from disappointments.

Chapter 9

George worked hard! For three months, in many towns and cities along the way, George did laundry, pitched hay, took care of animals—any job he could find. He knew he must save his money and plan well if he was going to make it through the winter. Do you think all of his jobs were fun or interesting? Probably not, but George knew the importance of **working hard**. In Colossians 3:23, our Heavenly Father tells us to work with all our heart at whatever job is placed before us—even if it isn't our favorite thing. He tells us that when we work, we are doing it to the glory of God, not other people. We must always keep this in mind. From things as little as chores around the house and caring for our siblings, to our careers we will have when we get older— we must work with all our hearts for the Lord and bring happiness to His heart!

Chapters 10-11

George writes to Mrs. Milholland and tells her he believes God has work for him to do. Therefore, he must take care of his health. He understands that even though God gives us grace and helps us, it is important to respect our bodies so we **stay healthy** for His plans for us! Read with your student 1 Corinthians 3:16, where the Lord tells us our bodies are living temples—where God's Spirit lives. Even the basics like brushing our teeth, going to bed at a reasonable hour and eating healthy meals are ways we can keep our bodies (and the Lord's temple!) strong and ready to serve. The Lord loves you and has work for you to do, just like George. Honor Him each day by taking care of the body He has given you!

1 Corinthians 3:16

Chapter 12

Dr. Carver and his students worked hard to complete their beautiful new brick agriculture building. Imagine how difficult it must have been to make those bricks, each by hand! The students, however, knew when their building was completed the hard work would be well worth the price. Can you imagine working even more grueling hours, for no wages, with no rewarding goal in mind? The Israelite slaves under Pharaoh did just that. Day in and day out they were forced to **make bricks** out of straw and clay for the myriad of buildings in Pharaoh's domain. Share with your student the story of the bricks without straw, located in Exodus 5:1-21.

Exodus 5:1-21

Moses and Aaron, called by God to free His people, go to Pharaoh and tell him the Lord has said to let His people go. Pharaoh not only scoffs at the two men, but becomes angry. He decides to make the work for the Israelite slaves even more difficult. Instead of requiring them to build a certain number of bricks each day with the supplied clay and straw, he will ask them to build that same number of bricks and gather their own straw! The Israelite slaves were stunned! How could they possibly complete their work quota each day, while being forced to go and gather the straw and stubble them selves? Instead of being thankful for Moses and Aaron's attempt to free them, the slaves became frustrated and angry with them. They didn't believe they would be freed—and now their job was even more difficult!

Five in a Row Bible Supplement

Exodus 13

Encourage your student's belief in God's faithfulness by sharing with him the rest of the story. In the end, God did free His people from the bondage of Pharaoh (Exodus 13). This tale of redemption shows how God responds to His children who, knowing their weaknesses, trust Him as their one true hope.

Chapter 13

The students in the School of Agriculture at Tuskegee knew their teacher, Dr. Carver, was extremely knowledgeable regarding insects and plant life. By creating a fake insect, they tried to trick him. Dr. Carver was too smart for them, however, and answered their query with an even wittier response. In the Bible, Jesus became the **wisest teacher** the earth had ever known. His followers and disciples were constantly amazed at His knowledge and wisdom. One day, the Pharisees decided to try to stump Jesus (Matthew 22:34-46). They asked Him what the greatest commandment was, thinking it would be impossible for Him to answer. Instead, Jesus immediately told them that the greatest commandment is to love our Lord with all our hearts. And then He continued by giving them the second greatest commandment. Like Dr. Carver, Jesus was unable to be tricked. Jesus is the greatest teacher of all and we can never stop learning from His wise lessons!

Matthew 22:34-46

Chapter 14

Dr. Carver taught his students the old adage "**waste not, want not**." When you see an opportunity to save something and reuse it, you should always do so. Your student probably remembers the story in the Bible of Jesus feeding the 5,000 from five loaves of bread and two fish. You may wish to review this story, located in Matthew 14:13-21. One interesting side note to that story, however, occurs in verse 20. After everyone had eaten, the disciples went around and collected all of the leftovers. They didn't just let what was left stay scattered on the ground. Instead, they put the extras into baskets. And do you know there were twelve basketfuls left? What do you think the disciples did with the leftovers? The Bible doesn't tell us, but they might have used them to help feed the poor and destitute in their area. Or perhaps they used the extra food as their own meals for a few more days. We can't be sure, but we do know the food was not wasted

Matthew 14:13-21

and left on the ground to rot. Encourage your student to look for opportunities to be frugal.

Chapter 15

The students at Tuskegee were fortunate to have a teacher like Dr. Carver—someone who was willing to take the time to share his passion for and knowledge of nature. The Bible tells us that we know of God because of the world around us (Romans 1:19-20). Have you ever looked at a daisy and counted each petal? Or watched a mother bird take such specific and gentle care of her babies? Do you know that no two snowflakes are alike? Can you imagine that? The intricacy and beauty of the natural world is **evidence** that there is a master Designer. The Lord created each molecule, nerve ending, color in the rainbow, butterfly, gorilla, elephant and giant oak tree! No world like ours could have happened by chance. Our Heavenly Father created a wonderful earth for us to live in and in so doing, shows us each day that He is real. Take a moment and thank Him today for all He has given us.

Romans 1:19-20

Chapters 16-17

Dr. Carver woke up each **morning** at four o'clock and began his day with a walk in the gardens and a prayer to God. He said, "At no other time have I so sharp an understanding of what God means to do with me. When other folks are still asleep, I hear God best and learn His plan." One of the psalmists, King David, shared Dr. Carver's belief in prayer and mornings. In Psalm 5:3, he tells us about his time with the Lord in the morning. David's psalm tells us he liked to lay his requests before God in the morning and wait in expectation for the answers. Is God really closer to us in the morning than during other times in the day or night? Of course not. Our Heavenly Father is always near our side, watching over us and listening to our prayers. Sometimes, however, the stillness of early morning hours is a wonderful time to share with the Lord. Some morning when you wake up early, remember King David and Dr. Carver and enjoy some early morning quiet time with God.

Psalm 5:3

Chapters 18-19

Draw your student's attention to Carver's account of his conversation with God. Dr. Carver said he asked the Lord what the universe was made for, but God answered it was too much to know. Then he asked what man was made for, but again the Lord didn't answer. Finally, he asked to know why God made the peanut and the Lord granted him knowledge. Can we ever know all there is to know about the world? Certainly not. Most of life is kept secret from the human mind. The Lord has a wonderful, complex and divine plan for all things and we can never hope to understand it.

Job 38-39

Deuteronomy 29:29

In the book of Job (chapters 38-39), the Lord questions Job and asks him to stop and consider all the **wonders of the world**. Through a long and powerful speech, God explains to Job that there will always be unanswered questions. But the secrets that the Lord chooses to reveal to us each day can be our treasures for a lifetime. As it says in Deuteronomy 29:29, "The secret things belong to the Lord our God, but the things that are revealed belong to us and to our children forever..."!

Teacher's Notes

The *Teacher's Notes* are optional but provide a space for you to document which Bible verse you choose and any other discussion points, songs, verses or notes you wish to keep record of for your student.

THE STORY OF GEORGE WASHINGTON CARVER

Date:

Student:

Five in a Row **Bible Verse(s):**

☐ Memorized Verse(s) / Copywork

Character Trait or Life Lesson to apply:

Related Worship Songs/Hymns

Misc. Notes:

Have your student draw a picture or write a reflection on the Bible verse(s) in the space below.

Five in a Row Bible Supplement

The Cricket in Times Square

Teacher's Note: In 2022, the publisher of *The Cricket in Times Square* issued a revised and updated edition of this classic children's book. Where there are differences between the two editions, this will be indicated in the Bible lesson.

Chapter 1—Tucker

When Paul understands that Mario isn't selling very many papers, he buys one and even gives Mario more than it's worth. Being **generous** is an important part of being a loving Christian. Since we have been given such an amazing gift from God—the gift of salvation—we should never be greedy or stingy to others. In Proverbs 21:26, the Word tells us that the evil man covets and gathers his things greedily all day long, but the godly man gives and does not withhold. God also promises in Proverbs 28:27 that when we give above and beyond to others who are in need, we will be given the things we need in return. God wants us to have big hearts, willing to see when people are in need and willing to share with them what we have. What are some things you can do to be more generous? If you are already a giving person, pray that God will bring people into your life that you can help. If being generous is hard for you, ask God to open your heart and fill you with a desire to share.

Proverbs 21:26

Proverbs 28:27

Chapter 2—Mario

Mario is a good listener. He hears the small chirp of the cricket and goes to investigate. Jesus wants us to **listen** to His voice closely, as well. He wants to lead in us in godly, happy lives. By reading the Bible, praying and listening to His quiet voice, we can hear His desire for us. In John 10:27, Jesus says that His sheep hear His voice and they follow Him. In Deuteronomy 30:19-20, God tells us He wants us to listen to His voice and hold fast to Him. Instead of rushing through your day, take a few moments now and then to thank your Heavenly Father for what He has given to you. Praise Him and be quiet for a few moments to hear what He says to your heart.

John 10:27
Deuteronomy 30:19-20

Chapter 3—Chester

Chester Cricket was accidentally taken from his home in Connecticut. He didn't know where he was going or whom he would meet. How frightening! Chester was fortunate to land in a spot where he found friends so quickly.

As a Christian, when you go through a frightening time, is your fate determined by luck, or something more? We are blessed to have a Heavenly Father who loves us and **watches out for us**. God knows what our lives are like during each minute. When we are in danger, He protects us and guides us through. His care and love aren't dependent upon what we look like or what we've done. They are unconditional.

In the Bible, there is an especially beautiful and comforting psalm— Psalm 23. Your student may be familiar with the words, but read them again. The psalmist says that our Lord guides us to refreshing, safe places. He is with us even when we walk through frightening paths, and He protects us always. Think about God's care and protection and rest in the assurance of His love for you. You are precious in His sight!

Psalm 23

Chapter 4—Harry Cat

Sometimes life seems hard, doesn't it? Everybody has days where nothing seems to go right. Chester Cricket certainly had a day like that when he got caught in a picnic basket and was whisked away from his home. But sometimes **good things** come out of bad circumstances, and the Bible talks about this very thing. In Romans 8:28, the apostle Paul writes that because we are children of God, all things will work together for good according to His will. This doesn't mean everything will always be great, but it does remind us that God's will is always going to be done. Next time you feel frustrated by a situation, remember God's promise to bring good out of all things.

Romans 8:28

Chapter 5—Sunday Morning

Mario takes very good care of his new friend Chester. He makes sure he has enough to eat and drink, and he watches over him carefully. The Bible is filled with discussions about **animals**. Take some time to explore some of these stories today. In Genesis 2:19-20, the Lord told Adam to name each of the animals in

Genesis 2:19-20

Five in a Row Bible Supplement

the Garden of Eden. Imagine how much creativity and excitement filled Adam as he tackled this assignment!

Matthew 6:25-27

In Matthew 6:25-27, Jesus talks about birds and their behavior. He tells us to watch the wonders of God's creation. Instead of worrying so much about material things, trust God for your needs just as His creation does!

Proverbs 12:10

The Bible also reminds us that we must be kind to our animals (Proverbs 12:10). Like Mario took care of Chester, it is important to treat animals with care. Owners must take care of their needs and think about what is best for them.

As you study God's Word, you will find that He loves all of creation. Mario is an excellent example of how we are supposed to behave.

Chapter 6—Sai Fong

Teacher's Note: In the 2022 revision of this book, Chapter 6 is "Mr. Fong" and the curio shop is a musical instrument shop.

When Mario visits Mr. Fong's shop, he sees little figurines of different goddesses in the glass case. Many people in the world do not practice Christianity. Instead of believing in one God, they believe in many gods and goddesses. As Christians, we know there is only one true God. He is the Creator of the universe. He sent His Son to Earth to die for our sins and to save us! He loves us more than anyone else in the world does.

Matthew 19:17
1 Corinthians 8:4
Exodus 34:27-28
Isaiah 9:6-7
Revelation 1:8

In God's Word, we read that there is only One who is good—God (Matthew 19:17). The Bible also tells us very clearly that idols aren't real, but there is only one God (1 Corinthians 8:4). We are so blessed, as children of God, to have both a strong and powerful God, but also a God who is gentle, loving and in control of our lives. Read more verses about our one true God: Exodus 34:27-28, Isaiah 9:6-7 and Revelation 1:8.

Chapter 7—The Cricket Cage

For a mouse (or a cricket), Chester's new pagoda was quite splendid. Tucker says, "You could feel like a king living in a place like this." Our Lord Jesus is a King, but He came to Earth as a man. When He was born as a baby, He didn't sleep in such fine quarters. Instead, He slept in a feeding trough full of hay!

Read with your student the story of Christ's birth (Luke 2) and think about how strange it would be to sleep where animals feed and sleep. Our beds are much nicer than that! God loved us so much that He sent His Son to Earth, to be born and then to be crucified for our sins (John 3:16). Jesus' time on Earth wasn't pleasant—beginning with His uncomfortable bed in the manger. But He came. He loved us. And He saved us. When you lay in your comfortable bed this evening, think about God's pleasure in and love for you. Think about Jesus' **willingness to be uncomfortable** for you, so you could always be His!

Luke 2

John 3:16

Chapter 8— Tucker's Life Savings

Chester has made a terrible mistake. He has accidentally eaten some of the Bellinis' money. Tucker encourages him to hide the fact or leave before anybody pins the incident on him. But Chester knows that would be **dishonest**. He is nervous about what Mama Bellini might do, but he knows being honest is more important than anything else. Chester is an honorable cricket!

We, too, as Christians, must work hard at being honest at all times. It is one of the Ten Commandments God gave: "You shall not bear false witness against your neighbor" (Exodus 20:16). Why does God ask us to be honest? He knows it will make our hearts softer and more pure before Him. He also knows it will keep our relationships healthier. When we lie to others, we hurt them and ourselves. God wants us to be as happy and blessed as possible, and He understands that lying only brings destruction. The next time you are tempted to tell a lie, think about Chester and how brave he was in his honesty. Being truthful takes bravery, but it will bring you happiness in the end!

Exodus 20:16

Chapter 9—The Chinese Dinner

Teacher's Note: In the 2022 revision of this book, Chapter 9 is "Supper with Mr. Fong."

Sai Fong is a good friend to Mario. Even though they are a somewhat unlikely pair, they are respectful and kind, and enjoy one another's company.

In the Bible, we read about being a **good friend** to others. God wants us to be loving, gentle and encouraging to the people around us. He also understands how special friends can become. He even says that some friends can be as close as brothers or sisters (Proverbs 18:24). Read the following verses about being a godly friend, and remember that the greatest friend of all is Jesus: Proverbs 17:17, 27:6 and 27:10.

Proverbs 18:24
Proverbs 17:17
Proverbs 27:6
Proverbs 27:10

Chapter 10—The Dinner P arty

Chester has a very special gift—the talent of musical ability. We all have special talents. Even if your gift isn't musical, God has given you **special abilities** all your own. God gives us talents for a reason. He longs for us to use them for a good purpose—to minister to and encourage other people and to give Him glory!

Matthew 25:14-30

There is a parable Jesus tells in the Bible about some men and their special gifts from God. It is found in Matthew 25:14-30. Jesus tells the story like this. One day a man was about to take a long trip. He called some of his servants together and told them he wanted them to watch over his property and take care of his money while he was gone. To one of the men he gave five pieces of money (the money was called "talents"). To the next man he gave two talents, and to the last he gave one talent. He told each of the men to use their money the best they could while he was away.

The man with the most money immediately began trading and conducting business deals and he quickly doubled his money. The second man, with two talents, also started working hard with the money and he, too, doubled what his master had given him. But the man with only one talent, thinking such a small amount would not be of much use, buried his money in a hole until his master returned home.

When the man of the house got back from his trip he was pleased to see that his first two servants had used their gifts and gained more. He told each of them he trusted them with a little, and now he would trust them with more. But to the servant who had buried his one talent, the master said he was ashamed. He was angry that his servant hadn't even tried to use the money for good.

Our Heavenly Father has given each of us real "talents." It doesn't matter if you think you're not special or you don't have a valuable gift. Whatever you are talented in brings God pleasure. He wants you to use your talents with all of your heart. In the end, it will bring joy to your heart and please the Lord.

Chapter 11—The Jinx

In this chapter's lessons, you learned about **exaggeration**. Some people don't think exaggerating the truth "a little" is really being dishonest. But it is, isn't it? The Lord longs for our hearts to be pure and blameless. He doesn't want anything to come between our hearts and Him. In the Bible, it tells us quite plainly that lying is wrong. In fact, in Colossians 3:9, the Bible says we should never lie to one another.

Colossians 3:9

Sometimes, the temptation to exaggerate is strong. Discuss these situations with your student or have him think of more: If you're telling your friend how far you ran in a race, it might be tempting to say it was just a little longer than it really was. Or if you're discussing a poor grade you received, it would be hard not to say it was a little better than it really was, wouldn't it? When you feel like exaggerating, remember what God says to us in Proverbs 12:19 and 22. He says that lying lips are an abomination to Him, but those who speak truthfully are His delight. If you fall into temptation and lie or exaggerate, then the Lord is quick to forgive you if you ask, and will always love you. So if you want to bring Him delight and if your heart wants to be pure and happy, ask for His help to avoid even small lies. His plans for you are great—don't put barriers in your way by dealing dishonestly with people. (Leviticus 19:11, Psalm 101:7 and Jeremiah 7:4)

Proverbs 12:19 & 22

Leviticus 19:11
Psalm 101:7
Jeremiah 7:4

Chapters 12-15—Mr. Smedley, Fame, Orpheus, and Grand Central Station

Mr. Smedley teaches music and voice lessons. Singing and opera are his favorite thing—his passion. Do you **sing** to the Lord? Worship and praise songs are one way our Heavenly Father loves to hear us communicate with Him! Singing of our love and praise makes His heart glad. Think of all He has done for you. Isn't it wonderful to know you can give something back?

Psalm 30:4
Psalm 47:6
Psalm 59:16
Psalm 89:1
Psalm 101:1
Ephesians 5:19

The book of Psalms is really a book of songs. King David and other psalm writers wrote these praise songs during Biblical times. Even if you feel silly for a moment, it might be fun to pick a psalm and sing it to the Lord during your devotional time or with your family. Make up a tune and let the Lord listen to your song. Here are some verses that talk about singing: Psalms 30:4, 47:6, 59:16, 89:1, 101:1 and Ephesians 5:19.

Teacher's Notes

The *Teacher's Notes* are optional but provide a space for you to document which Bible verse you choose and any other discussion points, songs, verses or notes you wish to keep record of for your student.

THE CRICKET IN TIMES SQUARE

Date:

Student:

Five in a Row Bible Verse(s):

☐ Memorized Verse(s) / Copywork

Character Trait or Life Lesson to apply:

Related Worship Songs/Hymns

Misc. Notes:

Have your student draw a picture or write a reflection on the Bible verse(s) in the space below.

Five in a Row Bible Supplement

Neil Armstrong: Young Flyer

Chapter 1—The Tin Goose

Neil is so excited when he hears about the Ford Tri-Motor. What a wonderful thing to see! Neil's father and mother know how much he wants to ride on the airplane. Imagine how thrilling it would be for Neil. Neil's father discusses how the plane will probably leave town very soon. Instead of being angry and nagging his parents, Neil is quiet. His mother sees his disappointment, but Neil doesn't say anything. In the end, his parents choose to allow Neil to go earlier and he is thrilled!

Deuteronomy 5:16

Matthew 7:7-11

Neil honors his parents by being respectful when he thinks he won't get what he wants. The Lord teaches us to **honor our parents** in all things (Deuteronomy 5:16). It is one of the Ten Commandments. But in return, what does God promise? Our Heavenly Father loves to give good things to his children. If we obey His commandments and laws, He promises to watch over us and give us good things. Sometimes they aren't always the things we want (like the ride in the Tri-Motor), but they are the things He knows are best for us. Read with your student the passage found in Matthew 7:7-11. In this passage, the Bible tells us that even though our parents love us, God loves us even more. He longs to **give us good things**. What a good Father we have!

Chapter 2—The First Plane

Ephesians 5:25

In this chapter, we learn about the abdication of King Edward VIII. The king left his throne because he desired to marry a woman who had been divorced. **Divorce** is not an easy thing to talk about. When two people who are married leave one another and are no longer married, everyone involved feels pain and sadness. Divorce between adults and parents sometimes happens. People are human and can make mistakes. But remember, divorce is never God's ideal plan for His children. The Lord wants us to have love in our lives and peace in our relationships. He desires our marriages to be full and happy. What does the Bible say about being married? In Ephesians 5:25 God tells us that husbands should love their wives as God loves us! Wives should love and honor their husbands, just as they honor and serve the Lord. Isn't that amazing? When we are married, we are supposed to look to the Lord as our model.

If you know someone who has felt the pain of divorce, remember that sad things happen, but God is a loving and forgiving God. If you would like, take a moment today and pray for the marriages of those you love. Ask the Lord to keep their marriage full of love and to give them strength and grace.

Chapter 3—A Special Trip

Neil's mother is a woman who is **content**. She is satisfied and happy with her life. Instead of worrying about the things she doesn't have, she focuses on all her blessings. What does the Bible say about being content? In Philippians 4:11, the apostle Paul tells the churches in Philippi he is learning to be content. Wherever he finds himself, he stays constant in his love for God and his faith in Him. Being content is about focusing on the good things you have. Our Heavenly Father loves you unconditionally and wants the best for you. You will find yourself to be more content if you spend time thanking Him for all the good things in your life.

Philippians 4:11

Chapter 4—Great Grandfather Koetter

The Armstrong children take turns riding a pony. Each of the children loves to ride, but they obey their father and share. **Sharing** is hard sometimes. When we are playing with something, or working on a project, it's easy to get selfish and think only about ourselves. When do you find it the hardest to share? The Bible talks a lot about putting others before ourselves. In fact, it is part of God's command to love our neighbor as ourselves (Leviticus 19:18). When you find it hard to share, remember this—sharing is something the Lord asks us to do. When we obey Him, our hearts grow softer and more able to hear His voice. If a sibling or friend wants a turn, then happily share. Not only are you giving her happiness, but you're obeying God and delighting His heart as well!

Leviticus 19:18

Chapter 5—The Wolf Patrol

Even when food was rationed, Neil's mother created good meals. The Lord **always provides** for His children. Sometimes it isn't exactly what we thought

1 Kings 17:8-16 we would get, but the Lord always provides! Share with your student the story of Elijah and the widow, found in 1 Kings 17:8-16. Elijah was told by God to go into the town of Zarephath. This area was going through a severe drought and famine. God told Elijah that He had commanded a widow in that town to care for him. When he got to Zarephath, he met the widow God commanded, but she only had enough supplies left for one more meal. After that, she and her son would begin to starve. But Elijah encouraged the widow. He told her not to fear and had her make enough of a meal for the three of them. He promised her that the Lord would not allow her lamp to run out of oil or her jar to run out of flour until He sent rain on the land. The Lord was faithful! No matter how much oil she used or how much flour she used in baking, there was always some left for many days! Encourage your student that no matter what happens, our Heavenly Father is faithful to care and provide for us.

Chapter 6—Camping Out

Neil, Bud and Kotchko all wanted to build the campfire, but the boys compromised and worked out a fair resolution. When we act unselfishly and choose to be **peacemakers** rather than picking a fight, then we act in a manner which makes the Lord happy. In the Bible, there is a book called Proverbs. Proverbs is filled with wonderful nuggets of truth—little reminders for how to lead a peaceful, godly life. Look in chapter 17 of Proverbs at the very first verse. **Proverbs 17:1** This verse talks about peace in our homes. Memorize this tiny proverb and tuck it in your heart. The next time you are given a situation where you can either fight or peacefully compromise, choose the latter. You will be making your Heavenly Father smile!

Chapter 7—A Scout's Pace

At the end of chapter 7 we read about Neil going back to the bakery at a "scout's pace," which is a combination of jogging and walking. His friends are surprised that Neil can do a 20-mile hike, use this scout's pace all the way to the bakery and then still have enough energy to work there!

Isaiah 40:29-31 Discuss with your student Isaiah 40:29-31, where the Lord tells us He will **give us strength**. The Bible tells us in this passage God will help us "run and not be weary, walk and not faint." Does this mean He will literally help us to run faster? We might run faster. But it probably means that when we get tired spiritually, He will renew our souls. Do you ever get tired spiritually? You may not have prayed for awhile and you're not even sure God is still listening. Everybody gets worn down sometimes. Satan works hard at frustrating us and he wants us to doubt the faithfulness of God. But the Lord promises that if we ask, He will energize and renew our strength. He will bring peace to our hearts and will help us keep going. In Hebrews 12:1, we are encouraged to run with endurance the race set before us. In His goodness and awesome sovereignty, the Lord promises to help us do just that—even when we think there is no way!

Hebrews 12:1

Chapter 8—Winners and Losers

When Neil saw the camera Bud and Kotchko were forced to make on the spur of the moment, he was a little surprised. It didn't look very good to him. He could tell they had rushed. Instead of thinking about how hard it must have been to have a project fail and try to replace it quickly, Neil seemed a little prideful. He didn't even say he was sorry to his friends for their misfortune. Instead, he quickly went back to working on his great steam turbine. Was this kind, godly behavior? It was neither kind nor godly behavior. In Proverbs 16:18, the Lord tells us that when we have **pride** in our heart, we fall. Neil seemed quite confident he would win a superior prize in the science fair. By all accounts, it would seem so, wouldn't it? But that did not happen.

Proverbs 16:18

At the last moment, Neil's project failed and the judges awarded Bud and Kotchko's little camera the top award. Sometimes the Lord reminds us of our pride by setting us in our place. Neil certainly got a reminder! Instead of feeling resentful, allow humbling experiences to be a reminder of God's desire that we be kind and loving people. He knows what is best for us! Other verses which talk about pride and humility include: Proverbs 15:33, 18:12, Isaiah 66:2, Daniel 4:28-33, Matthew 23:12, James 4:6 and 1 Peter 5:5.

Proverbs 15:33
Proverbs 18:12
Isaiah 66:2
Daniel 4:28-33
Matthew 23:12
James 4:6
1 Peter 5:5

Chapter 9—Another New School

Learning more about **the heavens** has been a focus in chapter 8 lessons. God, in His awesome way, has created a beautiful and stunning backdrop for our planet. No scientist knows how many stars are actually in the skies, but God does. He made each one and set it spinning in its place. He holds all the galaxies in His hands! Why not take some time to read in God's Word about the skies. The Bible is filled with references to the heavens. Look at Psalm 89:11 and Isaiah 66:1. Walk outside tonight and gaze up. Think about how wonderful your Heavenly Father is and how much He loves you. Then read more in His Word about the skies: Jeremiah 31:37, Psalm 19:1, 73:25, 103:11, Revelation 21:1.

Psalm 89:11
Isaiah 66:1
Jeremiah 31:37
Psalm 19:1
Psalm 73:25
Psalm 103:11
Revelation 21:1

Chapter 10—Flying Lessons

In chapter 10, we read that one of Neil's friends has died in a plane crash. Death is not easy to talk about. Sometimes it can make us feel very uncomfortable. Reading in God's Word, however, always brings comfort. Ecclesiastes 3:1-4 talks about everything in the world having its own time. God knows what is happening to everyone, all the time. When something happens that we don't understand, we can take comfort in God's Word. There is a time for everything. Even if it doesn't make sense to us, we can rest in the knowledge of God's guiding hand.

Ecclesiastes 3:1-4

Our Heavenly Father also desires to hold us and comfort us when we mourn and grieve the loss of someone. In Job 5:11 we read about God lifting those who mourn to safety. And in Psalm 30:11 the psalmist praises God for turning his mourning into dancing. More verses about **death or mourning** include Nehemiah 8:9, Jeremiah 31:13, Matthew 5:4 and Revelation 21:4.

Job 5:11
Psalm 30:11
Nehemiah 8:9
Jeremiah 31:13
Matthew 5:4
Revelation 21:4

Chapter 11—Airplanes to Astronauts

Neil was **brave** in battle. Being brave isn't always easy, but as Christians we have special help in this area. We have the Lord on our side! God promises to strengthen us in times of fear, and give us brave hearts to face the world. In Deuteronomy 31:6, God commands us to be strong and brave. God would never ask us to do something we couldn't do. With the help of the Holy Spirit,

Deuteronomy 31:6

you can face anything. To see this demonstrated, reread the story of David and Goliath (1 Samuel 17). To defeat a giant with only a sling and five small stones is a miracle! Only God could help David do such a thing. Only God could give David the courage to be brave enough to try it. When you are feeling particularly fearful, ask specifically for God to give you extra courage. He promises to help those who put their trust in Him.

1 Samuel 17

Chapter 12—Successes and Failures

Neil was very blessed to remain safe during both the Gemini 8 docking and the LLRV crash. Angels were most certainly protecting him and God was watching. **God protects** us, too. Open your Bible and read the story about Shadrach, Meshach and Abednego in the fiery furnace. Located in Daniel, chapter 3, we read that King Nebuchadnezzar has created a huge golden image and commands all to worship it. Everyone in the land worships the idol, except three men named Shadrach, Meshach and Abednego. They know it is wrong to serve any other god besides the one true God, so they refuse. The king is so enraged that he commands the three men to be thrown into a fiery furnace. Shadrach and his friends say they know the Lord can protect them, even in the fiery flames, but even if He chooses not to, they won't worship idols. When the king looks in the furnace, he is amazed! There are four men walking around in the flames, unharmed! Shadrach, Meshach and Abednego are fine! When the king sees this, he realizes he has been wrong and releases them. He then commands his subjects to worship their God. We have a loving, faithful Father who protects, even when all seems lost.

Daniel 3

Chapter 13—Preparations

Preparing for something means getting things ready, making sure everything is perfect before the event takes place. Do you know that God is preparing a place for us? He is! In John 14:1-3, Jesus is getting ready to leave His disciples. The disciples are very upset. Jesus tells them He is going to go and provide a place for them. God has, in His amazing way, planned a heaven for us to go to when we leave this earth. He has created a perfect paradise, preparing for us and planning each detail. Think about God's goodness and read more verses about His prepa-

John 14:1-3

Five in a Row Bible Supplement

rations just for you! Some verses are Matthew 22:4, 25:34 and 1 Corinthians 2:9.

Chapter 14—The First Man on the Moon

In chapter 14, President Nixon tells the astronauts, "...it inspires us to redouble our efforts to bring peace and tranquility to Earth". What is "peace"? Webster's dictionary defines it as "freedom from strife of any kind; a quiet harmony." What does **peace** mean to you? Peace can mean many different things, but to us as Christians it can mean a resting faith in God. God loves us so much that He sent Jesus to die for our sins (John 3:16). When He did this, He made a way for us to be forgiven and a path for us to heaven, to be with Him. Resting in that can mean peace for our hearts.

The Bible tells us to pursue peace in our hearts (Psalm 34:14). It reminds us that if we love God and obey His laws, peace comes to us (Psalm 119:165). Peace is knowing that you are loved by a Heavenly Father who calls you His child. Peace is worshipping a Creator who knit you in your mother's womb (Psalm 139:13-14) and will always be by your side. Take a moment today and thank the Lord for giving you His heavenly peace—one which passes all understanding (Philippians 4:7). Here are more verses about peace for your study: John 14:27 and 16:33.

Chapter 15—A Hero's Welcome Home

The discussion in this final chapter centers around **completing goals**. Neil says that any goal is achievable, if you know what you're trying to do and you work with others. As Christians, what can we add to that statement? We can add "with God's help!" All things are possible through our Lord Jesus Christ (Matthew 19:26). Isn't that a comforting and exciting thought? You have a loving, powerful God and an army of angels on your side! When you are striving toward a goal, God can strengthen and refresh you. He can bring people into your life to help you. He can encourage you when you're down. God loves you and is very interested in everything you're doing. Talk to Him about what you're feeling and what you're trying to accomplish. He will hear you and answer! Other verses about God helping us achieve more are Mark 9:23 and Luke 18:27.

Matthew 22:4
Matthew 25:34
1 Corinthians 2:9

John 3:16

Psalm 34:14
Psalm 119:165

Psalm 139:13-14
Philippians 4:7
John 14:27
John 16:33

Matthew 19:26

Mark 9:23
Luke 18:27

Teacher's Notes

The *Teacher's Notes* are optional but provide a space for you to document which Bible verse you choose and any other discussion points, songs, verses or notes you wish to keep record of for your student.

NEIL ARMSTRONG: YOUNG FLYER

Date:

Student:

Five in a Row Bible Verse(s):

☐ Memorized Verse(s) / Copywork

Character Trait or Life Lesson to apply:

Related Worship Songs/Hymns

Misc. Notes:

Have your student draw a picture or write a reflection on the Bible verse(s) in the space below.

Five in a Row Bible Supplement

Marie Curie and the Discovery of Radium

Chapter 1—Small Beginnings

Manya's mother is very sick. Imagine how difficult it would be to have your mother never hug or kiss you good night, and not even know why! Even though she knows it probably confuses them, Mrs. Sklodowska does what she hopes is best for her children. She understands that her disease is contagious and they could become ill if she gets too close to them.

Sometimes, things happen in our lives that are confusing. We aren't sure what God's plan is and it makes us frustrated. Remember, just like Manya's mother, God is a loving Father who does what is best for His children! He has His reasons—things we don't understand or know. One way of describing God's attitudes and actions toward you is to say He is **faithful**. Being faithful means not letting someone down—always keeping His promises. He is faithful to love you and care for you. Look at these verses in God's Word and think about His faithfulness to you, even when you don't understand your situation: Psalm 33:4, 2 Timothy 2:13, Hebrews 10:23.

Psalm 33:4
2 Timothy 2:13
Hebrews 10:23

Chapter 2—The Painful Years

Manya doesn't understand why her mother died. She feels lonely and sad, and **mourns** for a long time. When Jesus died on the cross, His friends and family felt very much the same way. Even though He had warned them He would be leaving, they couldn't believe He was actually gone.

John 20:1-18

Read the story of Jesus' friend, Mary Magdalene, found in John 20:1-18. After Jesus is raised from the dead, his friends, Simon Peter, Mary and others go to see Him in the tomb. Of course, they don't find His body because He is already gone. His friends think His body was stolen. Mary's grief over the death of her Lord is deepened and she weeps for a long time. Miraculously, two angels appear to her and explain that Jesus is alive. And then Jesus appears to Mary. He explains to her that now He will be with her always. She will never be alone again.

Grieving and mourning the death of someone we love is a natural, important part of the healing process. As Christians, however, we can rest in the arms of our Heavenly Father who is always with us and comforts our hearts. Jesus longs to turn our mourning into joy—our sorrow into gladness (Jeremiah 31:13).

Jeremiah 31:13

Chapter 3—Growing Up

Manya unselfishly decides to help support and send her sister Bronya to Paris for college, before she goes herself. In the Bible we read that the first will be last and the last will be first (Mark 10:31). That seems backward, doesn't it?

Mark 10:31

As Christians, many things God asks us to do seem backward to the way others in the world act. People generally think if they work hard to get in ahead and in front of others, then they will be successful. Instead, Jesus asks us to **support other people** and encourage them in their lives, instead of pushing to surpass them. Manya's decision to wait on her own education in order to help her sister, is a godly decision. And the Lord will reward her.

Our Heavenly Father wants us to become unselfish servants, not pushy bosses. God's blessings are always going to be more rewarding than earthly wealth and success. The Beatitudes, found in Matthew 5, talk a lot about God's desire for our character and behavior. Read them with your student today, and talk about Manya's decision.

Matthew 5

Chapter 4—The Sacrifice

Manya has great hope that she has found the right person to spend the rest of her life with—Casimir. Imagine, after having to leave her father and family behind in order to work, how much Manya longed for companionship and family! Unfortunately, Casimir's family is backward in their thinking and believe that Casimir should only marry someone who is as rich as they are.

In Proverbs 13:12 we read that **a hope deferred** (put on hold) makes the heart grow sick, but a longing fulfilled is like a tree of life. Manya's heart certainly felt sick, didn't it? Jesus understands our needs and He longs to give us our heart's desire. Sometimes, however, what is best for us isn't what we want. God knows things we do not. He tells us to put our hope in Him, not in people or circum-

Proverbs 13:12

Psalm 42:5 stances (Psalm 42:5). God also wants us to have faith. Faith means believing
Hebrews 11:1 and hoping for things you can't see and verify (Hebrews 11:1). When you face disappointments, have faith and put your hope in God. He loves you!

Chapter 5—The Turning Point

Manya is finally attending the Sorbonne in Paris! She has worked hard and helped others first, but now her chance has come. Manya is a good example of a faithful person. She does what is right, and helps her family as much as she is able. The Bible is full of principles—things which are always true. One principle is that God **rewards the faithful**.

If you seek after the Lord with your heart and resolve to do what is right, the Lord will reward you greatly! Look at Psalm 19:9-11 and read what David says: The rules of the Lord are sure … in keeping them there is a great reward.

Psalm 19:9-11

Matthew 16:27 In Matthew 16:27, the Bible tells us that Jesus will come again to Earth and reward His children according to what they have done. Our Heavenly Father watches over us carefully, and delights when He sees us doing right. He prom-

1 Corinthians 3:14 ises to reward you. Read 1 Corinthians 3:14 with your student and think about God's faithfulness to us.

Chapter 6—A French Education

Our author tells us that Bronya's home was "full of love." Our Heavenly Father longs for each of His children to live in **houses full of love**. God doesn't want our hearts to hurt, or be angry. Instead, He asks us to reach out toward one another. He asks us to forgive quickly. He asks us to put others before ourselves.

Sometimes it can be difficult to act in a way that pleases God. We get frustrated and hurt, and all we want to do is hurt someone else. If we act on those feel-

Proverbs 10:12 ings, however, our homes will be full of strife—or fighting. In Proverbs 10:12,
Matthew 5:44 the Bible tells us that love can cover many wrongs. As you work toward filling
John 13:34, 14:15 your heart and your family's home with love, look over the following verses and
Romans 5:5 think about what you can do to add some love today! Matthew 5:44, John 13:34,
Ephesians 3:17 14:15, Romans 5:5 and Ephesians 3:17.

Chapter 7—Changes

Pierre and Marie fall in love and marry. Marie knows she has found the right person to spend the rest of her life with—someone whom she can relate to and love. In the Bible we read that God created the first couple— Adam and Eve. In Genesis 2, you can read about God's creation of human beings.

Genesis 2

God created Adam, but He soon realized something was missing. In verse 18, God talks about creating a helper for Adam. God understands it isn't right for Adam to be alone. In this special way, God gave Adam and Eve to one another.

Genesis 2:18

When you grow up, **finding the right mate** may seem a little tricky. There are so many people in the world. How do you know who is a "suitable helper" for you? Trust God and ask Him to bring the right person to you. Just like Pierre and Marie found one another, so God can bring the perfect person to you. The Lord delights in giving good things to His children, and nothing is too difficult for Him! (As a parent, you might consider relating the story of how God brought you and your spouse together before your student was born.)

Chapter 8—A Surprising Discovery

Marie has made an amazing discovery! She has discovered an unknown element. To Marie, the science community and the world, this new finding is quite a surprise. But is it a surprise to God? Of course not. God created the entire world, and He knows everything! Every element. Each fish in the sea. How many hairs you have on your head! How many freckles you have on your nose! God knows more than any human could ever know.

There is one thing, however, that only God can know. No matter how hard someone worked, or how much research was involved, no one can ever know **what is in your heart**. It is a great secret, and God holds the answer. Do you ever have those days where you just want to pound on the wall? Or you feel like crying, but don't because you're afraid someone might make fun of you. God understands and He sees inside your heart. He knows every feeling, thought and motive and He loves you deeply. In Psalm 139, David writes about God know-

Psalm 139

ing his every move; He even knows his heart. Read that psalm today and think about the surprise discovery no one but God can ever make—understanding your heart!

Chapters 9-11—More Discoveries, Four Hard Years, Awards and Sorrows

Marie and Pierre don't care about becoming wealthy from their scientific findings. They are more concerned about their work and helping others than gaining money. What do you think? Are there things in life more important than money?

As Christians, we know that money is just an earthly thing. We are spiritual creatures, and when we die we will go to heaven to be with God. In heaven, we won't have our earthly possessions or money. Instead, we will have eternal life. This eternal life—salvation—is worth far **more than money**.

Ephesians 2:7
Psalm 119:14
Proverbs 30:8
Isaiah 10:3
Matthew 19:23

In Ephesians 2:7, the Bible tells us that God's grace is worth incomparable riches. Grace and eternal life are the things of value for you—not money. Read more verses in the Bible about our heavenly riches and think about Marie and Pierre's decision: Psalm 119:14, Proverbs 30:8, Isaiah 10:3 and Matthew 19:23.

Chapter 12—Tragedy

Marie loses her husband, Pierre, in a tragic accident. She grieves for a long time and finds it difficult to go on. Death is a hard thing to deal with, isn't it? Losing someone we love can make us feel angry, depressed and lonely. As Christians, however, we have another way to look at **death**. For us, death is not an end, but a beginning!

John 3:16
John 3:36
John 5:24
Romans 6:23
Ecclesiastes 3:11

The Bible tells us that Jesus came and died for our sins (John 3:16), in order that we might receive a special gift if we believe. That special gift is eternal life! This means we will live forever with God and the angels in heaven (John 3:36, 5:24 and Romans 6:23). In Ecclesiastes 3:11, the Lord shows us that He has made everything on Earth. He controls everything and gives each event a specific time—even death. But God also reassures us that even though we don't understand His timing, we can know we will be with Him when we die. It says He has set eternity in our hearts. Eternity means forever!

So remember, even when you lose someone you love, God has a special plan and time. And for those who believe in Him, death is continuing life forever!

Chapters 13-15—Dreams and War, A Special Gift, The Final Years

Marie volunteers her time and helps during World War I. Wars are terrible conflicts which arise between two different groups of people. Did you know that there is always a conflict going on over us? Just like in a war, Satan and his messengers are constantly building "strategies" to tempt us do things which are wrong. They want us to fail. They plot and plan, hoping we will lie, act disrespectfully or selfishly and more.

On the other side of the "battle" are Jesus and His angels. God fights for us and with us, helping us overcome evil and act in a godly manner. Jesus longs for us to conquer Satan and come out the victor! God even gives us special **armor to use in battle**—just like a real soldier. In Ephesians 6:10-17, we learn about this suit of armor. Read over the passage and think about each piece: belt of truth, breastplate of righteousness, shoes of peace, shield of faith, helmet of salvation and the sword of the Spirit, which is the Word of God.

Ephesians 6:10-17

How do we put on this "armor"? By praying daily and reading the Bible. As we absorb and dwell on God's will for our lives, we will begin to overcome temptation and use our spiritual armor, which God gives us to help us succeed in every way! God loves us, protects us and gives us the tools we need to help defend ourselves.

Teacher's Notes

The *Teacher's Notes* are optional but provide a space for you to document which Bible verse you choose and any other discussion points, songs, verses or notes you wish to keep record of for your student.

MARIE CURIE AND THE DISCOVERY OF RADIUM

Date:

Student:

Five in a Row Bible Verse(s):

☐ Memorized Verse(s) / Copywork

Character Trait or Life Lesson to apply:

Related Worship Songs/Hymns

Misc. Notes:

Have your student draw a picture or write a reflection on the Bible verse(s) in the space below.

Hitty: Her First Hundred Years

Chapter One—"In Which I Begin My Memoirs"

Phoebe is working on a new dress for Hitty. Even though Phoebe is not an accomplished seamstress, Hitty tells us that the little girl worked diligently on the sewing project. **Diligence** can be easy when we are doing something we enjoy. Assembling a model airplane or baking a batch of cookies takes diligent effort, but it is fun! We find ourselves more challenged, however, when the project becomes difficult or it is something we don't enjoy.

As Christians, we look to our Heavenly Father and the Bible for instructions in our lives. The Bible clearly states that diligence (especially during difficult circumstances) is important to the heart of God. He understands our desire to take the easy road. However, He knows that if we are faithful to our duties and diligent in seeking Him, we will be happier and more satisfied. Look over the following verses and ask God to help you become more diligent: Proverbs 8:17, 10:4, 12:24 and 21:25.

Proverbs 8:17
Proverbs 10:4
Proverbs 12:24
Proverbs 21:25

Chapter Two—"In Which I Go Up in the World and Am Glad to Come Down Again"

In this chapter, we see Phoebe and Andy treating the five Native American wives in an ignorant and hurtful way. In the chapter lessons, we also learned about racism in our language and how destructive it can be. People who look **different from us** are just as valuable and loved by God as we are.

In Genesis 1, God created the first man and woman—Adam and Eve. Look at that reference (Genesis 1:27). The Bible tells us God created man (meaning every human) in His own image. It doesn't matter if someone has brown skin, white skin, red hair or blonde, blue eyes or brown—we are all made in the likeness of God. Learning to love people who are different not only shows them the love of God, but also enriches our lives immeasurably! Ask God to continually fill you with love and help you see everyone through His eyes.

Genesis 1:27

Five in a Row Bible Supplement

Chapter Three—"In Which I Travel—by Land and Sea"

In this chapter, Hitty is found and returned to the Prebles. They are excited to have her home. Phoebe and Andy spent hours looking for Hitty in the raspberry patch and when Andy spies her in the tree, the whole family works to save her.

Matthew 18:10-14

As Christians, we can relate to this story of **loss and recovery**. In Matthew 18:10-14, Jesus tells the parable of the lost sheep. In the story, a shepherd is tending his flock. He owns 100 sheep! Suddenly, the shepherd notices one lamb has wandered away from the flock and into the hills. Jesus tells us the shepherd leaves the 99 to search for the lost lamb until it is found. Jesus goes on to say the man is as happy about finding that one sheep as he is about the 99 who did not run away.

Like all parables, this story has a bigger message. Jesus tells us our Heavenly Father is like that shepherd. If we lose our way, he zealously seeks us out. He does not want even one of His children to be lost.

Remember this always—no one is too insignificant to be noticed in heaven. You are special and loved by God and He will always be watching over you!

Chapter Four—"In Which We Go to Sea"

Mrs. Preble is a devoted wife and mother. She is always as concerned with the family's spiritual needs as she is for their physical needs. Even though the Prebles are out on the high seas, far from their church, she continues to encourage them with passages from the Bible.

Psalm 23

In this chapter, we see Mrs. Preble reviewing one of the most beautiful passages in the Scriptures with her daughter—the 23rd Psalm. Read this passage. Consider what the words mean. This passage describes in a wonderful way how much God **cares** for us. He nourishes us spiritually and emotionally, as well as physically. He always provides the essential things we need. His loving care provides us with a peace in our lives. We can trust Him!

Perhaps it would be fun to write out this Psalm in calligraphy or in an interesting font on the computer. Then, using colored pencils, watercolors, crayons, etc., embellish the background and edges with pictures inspired by the verses. A green pasture or river perhaps. By hanging the finished piece near a bedside or table you can review and remind yourself of God's promises throughout the day. Mrs. Preble worked to keep God's promises close to her heart—you will find comfort by doing the same.

Chapter Five—"In Which We Strike Our First and Last Whale"

It was very sad when most of the crew on the *Diana-Kate* left the Prebles and dishonored their captain. Those crewmembers were not loyal friends.

In this chapter, we've discussed being **loyal**. Loyalty is not as common as it should be. In Proverbs 18:24, we read that each person may have many friends who don't stick by him, but there is a friend who sticks closer than a brother. Are you that kind of friend? Are you loyal and loving to those you spend time with? Have you ever had a friend who let you down? How did you feel?

Proverbs 18:24

Just as God asks us to be loyal and loving to others, He promises to be loyal to us. God is faithful. There is no one who cares more about you, watches after you more closely or promises to stand by you more than Him.

Chapter Six—"In Which I Join the Fishes and Rejoin the Prebles"

The natives in our story steal Hitty in order to make her their god or idol. As Christians we understand this is wrong. We believe in one, and only **one, true God**.

In Exodus 19-20, God appears to Moses and gives him the Ten Commandments, which Moses records on two stone tablets. He tells Moses to warn the people about making idols and altars to false gods. The Lord clearly says, "Do not worship any other god."

Exodus 19-20

We serve a mighty and jealous God. God's jealousy springs from love for us and what is best for us. He wants our exclusive love and devotion.

In your life today, you probably won't create an idol or an altar to a false god. At times, however, we all put other things before the Lord. For example, we may skip our prayer time because we're running late. Or we might keep all our money instead of tithing because we're saving up for something we really want. In these small ways, we are putting other things before God. Remember His commandments and strive to always put the one true God first in your heart and life.

Chapter Seven—"In Which I Learn the Ways of Gods, Natives, and Monkeys"

In this chapter, we explored the beauty and wonder of God's "glowing" animals. Bioluminescent creatures are just a small part of **God's creation**. Every mountain, star, animal and flower—indeed, everything ever created—shows us how diverse and artistic God is.

Psalm 104:24

In Psalm 104:24, the Bible tells us the earth is full of God's creatures. In His wisdom, he formed each one carefully and lovingly. God is the source of all life! As you think about this Bible lesson, why not take a walk and look at nature. Find something you find fascinating or beautiful (i.e., an acorn, leaf, flower, butterfly, etc.) and thank God for it. Looking at the world around us teaches us about our God, gives us awe for Him, and creates in us thankful hearts.

Chapter Eight—"In Which I Am Lost in India"

In one brief moment, Phoebe drops Hitty and suddenly everything changes, doesn't it? Without warning, Hitty is lost in India and the story tells us she never sees the Prebles again. Can life really take such unexpected dips and turns? Sometimes we forget how quickly things can **change**.

Your life has probably not been quite as dramatic as Hitty's, but you have experienced surprises—some pleasant and some sad. As humans, we want to know everything that is going to happen, don't we? It's fun to make plans for the future, and those plans would certainly be easier if we knew exactly what to expect. We don't, but God does.

In James 4:13-14, God reminds us that no one knows what tomorrow will bring. It's okay to make plans, but we should never believe that each thing we prepare for will happen just the way we want. It is good to be flexible.

For Hitty, we will see how this new turn of events works out. For you, pray today and ask God to direct your path. You can't know the future, but by trusting in your loving Heavenly Father you can rest in the knowledge that He knows and will lead you right where you are supposed to be. He is faithful.

In this chapter, we also looked at another kind of religion—Hinduism. One of the primary beliefs of that religion is that there are many gods. As Christians, we know that there is only one God. In Deuteronomy 6:4, the Bible says, "The Lord is our God, the Lord is One."

Hinduism also includes a belief in reincarnation—that each person has many lives. As Christians we know this isn't true either. In Hebrews 9:27 the Bible tells us that each person is destined to die once and face judgment, as Christ was sacrificed once and will appear again to save those who believe.

It is important as you look at different beliefs to always remember what *you* believe, weighing each thing you learn against the Word of God—the ultimate truth!

Chapter Nine—"In Which I Have Another Child to Play with Me"

Hitty tells us that she doesn't think Little Thankful ever lived up to her name. What does it mean to be **thankful**? Do you live up to that name?

If you are thankful or grateful, you are appreciative of what has been given to you. You understand the kindness behind the gift. When we are thankful, we want to give something back in return.

In 1 Thessalonians 5:16-18, the Bible reminds us to be joyful, to pray and to give thanks in all circumstances. Thankfulness is easy when we are having a wonderful day. When you are having a bad day, it is still important to find things you

James 4:13-14

Deuteronomy 6:4

Hebrews 9:27

1 Thessalonians 5:16-18

Five in a Row Bible Supplement

are thankful for and give God the glory. At first, it may seem hard. But in time, gratitude and thankfulness become second nature. You will be overflowing with thankfulness to God for so many things!

Ask God to build up your spirit today and increase your thankfulness—thankfulness in all circumstances!

Chapter Ten—"In Which I Am Rescued and Hear Adelina Patti" and Chapter Eleven—"In Which I Sit for My Daguerreotype and Meet a Poet"

Ruth Pryce is comforted when she finds out her beau, John Norton, is being cared for in a Southern hospital. She is thankful when John writes and tells her about a little Southern girl who brings him flowers and tries to cheer him up. Even though John Norton fights for the Yankee army, that little girl from the South understands his needs and does her best to help him get well.

Luke 10:25-37

In the Bible, we see a story about a man who is ailing (Luke 10:25-37). He has been traveling alone from Jerusalem to Jericho. Unfortunately, robbers attack him on the road. They beat him and leave him alone and dying. A little time later, a priest walks by the man, but he doesn't help. Then a Levite (a person of the priestly tribe) walks by, but he, too, chooses to leave the poor man. Both the priest and the Levite were supposed to be godly men—they should have shown some compassion. Finally, a Samaritan comes by and takes pity on the beaten man. Samaritans and Jews normally didn't even get along at that time, and yet this Samaritan takes the injured man to an inn (hotel), bandages his wounds and gives the innkeeper money to pay for the injured man's stay.

Jesus told this story as an example of how we are to **respond to those in need**. Just like the Samaritan and the little Southern girl, we are supposed to help those we see in need, regardless of who they are or from where they come. Today, ask God to open your heart and give you a greater sense of compassion for others.

Chapter Twelve—"In Which I Go Into Camphor, Reach New York, and Become a Doll of Fashion" and Chapter Thirteen—"In Which I Spend a Disastrous New Year's and Return to New England"

Isabella's parents tell her she is too young to attend the New Year's Eve festivities. Instead of listening to her parents' counsel and obeying their instruction, Isabella disobeys and goes anyway. When we're young, we often think we know more than our parents. We think their way is old fashioned and boring. If only we understood how wise they really are!

In Exodus 20:12, the Lord talks about **honoring your father and mother**. God doesn't desire that you obey just to take the fun out of your life. He longs for your life to be filled with joy and happiness! He knows that your parents have lived longer than you and He has given them special wisdom in how to raise you. They love you more than anyone else on earth. Their hope is for you to live a long and fulfilled life, and they will do all they can to help you on that path. If you disobey them and ignore their advice (like Isabella), you are not only disobeying God, but you are cheating yourself of all your parents' advice and experience. They've been there before and they have probably made many mistakes. Listen to them. Learn from them. Use your parents as a sounding board for your ideas and plans. If they think it's a great idea, chances are it truly is and it will be good for you. If they are against it, obey the Lord, listen to them and wait. You will likely be amazed at what happens. Many times, if we only will obey, we are spared sadness and problems.

Exodus 20:12

The next time you are asking for something and your parents disagree with you, take a deep breath and listen to their argument. Find out their reasoning and, even if you don't understand it, take their advice. You will not only be helping yourself, you'll be blessing them and pleasing your Heavenly Father.

Chapter Fourteen—"In Which I End My Hay-Days and Begin a New Profession" and Chapter Fifteen—"In Which I Learn Much of Plantations, Post Offices, and Pin Cushions"

These chapters revealed two very different sorts of people. Sally Loomis was dishonest and sinful in her behavior with Hitty. She stole the doll from the Exposition and, instead of confessing her wrongdoing, she simply threw Hitty into the river. Miss Hope, on the other hand, truly displayed honesty and godly character when she explained to Car'line that Hitty belonged to someone else. Even when Miss Hope decided she herself liked Hitty, she was "true to her convictions" and returned Hitty to her rightful owners.

John 14:6
Proverbs 23:23

We can learn so much from Miss Hope's actions. The Bible tells us that God desires us to be people of our word. We also know that the Lord longs for us to be people who are **truthful** with ourselves and others. In fact, Jesus even tells us He is "the way, the truth, and the life" (John 14:6). In Proverbs 23:23 we read, "Buy truth and do not sell it..." Sometimes when we want something so much, we don't want to be completely honest and right about what we are doing. Just like Sally, we sometimes lie to ourselves and others if we want something badly enough. Each and every day we should strive to be more like Miss Hope—knowing what is right and doing it, even when we wish we could do something else. It isn't always easy to be truthful, but when we do what is right we please our Father in heaven and we keep ourselves on the right path.

Chapter Sixteen—"In Which I Return to Familiar Scenes" and Chapter Seventeen—"In Which I Am Sold at Auction", "And Last Remarks"

Did you know that each and every one of us has a specific and awesome purpose? God created you with love and attention to detail. He carefully formed your body—paying attention to your hair, your eyes ... every inch of you—right down to your individual fingerprints and cell structure! Along with your physical makeup, God also created your emotional makeup. He knows just what makes you laugh. He knows why you're sensitive in certain areas. But most importantly, God created you with an **individual purpose**. God gives each of us talents and gifts and He longs for us to make use of them. Sometimes it takes a while to discover what you're good at. Some people are writers and others are farmers; some are presidents of companies and some are manual laborers. God knows exactly what gift He gave to you and He can't wait for you to use it for His glory.

The Bible reminds us that each person has her own gifts from God. What are your gifts? What do you think God's purpose is for you? Read these verses from the Bible that discuss purpose and gifts: Psalms 57:2 and 138:8, Romans 8:28, Romans 12:5-7, 1 Corinthians 12. As long as you follow the Lord, seek His heart and ask Him. He is faithful to lead you in the right path. Follow your Heavenly Father and you will discover your special purpose.

Psalm 57:2
Psalm 138:8
Romans 8:28
Romans 12:5-7
1 Corinthians 12

Five in a Row Bible Supplement

Teacher's Notes

The *Teacher's Notes* are optional but provide a space for you to document which Bible verse you choose and any other discussion points, songs, verses or notes you wish to keep record of for your student.

HITTY: HER FIRST HUNDRED YEARS

Date:

Student:

Five in a Row **Bible Verse(s):**

☐ Memorized Verse(s) / Copywork

Character Trait or Life Lesson to apply:

Related Worship Songs/Hymns

Misc. Notes:

Have your student draw a picture or write a reflection on the Bible verse(s) in the space below.

Helpful Bible Study Materials:

For Parents:

What the Bible is All About by Dr. Henrietta C. Mears. This well-loved classic Bible handbook looks at each book of the Bible and offers outlining and insights in a delightful way. It is currently available in a revised and updated edition for more than one Bible translation.

The New Strong's Expanded Exhaustive Concordance of the Bible by James Strong is an excellent print concordance. You can also use websites like biblegateway.com to search for certain words, verses, etc.

Hymns of Faith by Tabernacle Publishing Company

Trinity Hymnal by Great Commission Publications

Parents Resource Bible: A Life Application Bible (*The Living Bible*), Tyndale House Publishing

Celebrating Biblical Feasts In Your Home or Church by Martha Zimmerman

For Children:

Rose Book of Bible Charts, Maps, and Time Lines is a bestselling resource that includes reproducible Bible reference material for the whole family, especially older children and teens through adults.

International Children's Bible Field Guide by Lawrence Richards. Includes Bible stories, character sketches, geography, archaeology, customs and spiritual truths, with simple definitions and explanations of Biblical words, phrases and events.

Wee Sing Bible Songs and *Wee Sing More Bible Songs*, available digitally or in book/CD sets with words, music, and chords. (For younger children)

The New Bible in Pictures for Little Eyes by Kenneth N. Taylor has sold more than 1.5 million copies and has been translated into at least 70 languages. Each page has a richly colored picture and a very brief Bible story. (For younger children)

Afterword

We hope that you have found some helpful Bible selections and have enjoyed using the *Five in a Row Bible Supplement* along with your curriculum. Remember that these verses and ideas are only suggestions and there are many other ways to incorporate Biblical principles into your studies. We leave you, the teacher, with this passage from Isaiah 54:13: "All your children shall be taught by the Lord, and great shall be the peace of your children." May the Lord richly bless you in all your teaching.

Jane Claire Lambert
March 1997, July 2021

Index

A

Accomplishment, 110
Advice, 33
Allegiance, 28
Animal care, 9
Animals, 16, 97
Armor, 117
Authority, 28

B

Bartimaeus, 75
Battles, 55
Bible, 26
Birth of Jesus, 80
Bitterness, 20
Boast, 41
Bravery, 108
Bread of Life, 8
Bricks, 91

C

Christianity, 98
Christmas, 77
Church, 88
Coins, 23
Cold, 18
Comfort, 44, 47
Communion, 20
Confidence, 51
Contentment, 105
Creation, first day, 8

D

Dancing, 56
David, 39
Death, 116
Delegate, 54
Differences, 22, 88, 119
Diligence, 53, 119
Discipline, 75
Dishonest, 99
Disobedience, 71
Divorce, 104
Doubt, 76
Drought, 82

E

Evidence, 93
Exaggeration, 101

F

Faithful, 90, 112, 114
Family, 59
Fear, 10
Fire, 82
Flowers, 60
Friend, 100
Frightened, 72

G

Generous, 68, 96
Gifts, 13
God's creation, 122
God's love, 11
Good Samaritan, 36, 67, 124
Great Commission, 63
Greatest commandment, 12
Greed, 11

H

Heal, 25
Health, 91
Heavens, 108
Honor, 70, 104
Hope, 24, 65, 66, 81
Humble, 40

I

Integrity, 37

K

Kindness, 67, 84

L

Lamp, 39
Letters, 84
Light, 56
Listen, 96
Loaves and fish, 92
Lord's Supper, 20
Loss, 120
Love, 27, 34, 80
Loyal, 121

M

Manna, 88
Marriage, 21, 59, 115
Meals, 33
Meditate, 25
Mercy, 52
Modesty, 85
Morning, 93
Mourning, 108, 112
Move, 51
Music, 71, 83

N

Natural world, 18
Neighbors, 52, 61
Noah's ark, 62

O

Obey, 50, 70

P

Parable of the two sons, 36
Parents, 125
Peace, 110
Peacemaker, 106
Perseverance, 12, 78
Persistent, 41
Pillar of fire, 83
Polite, 48
Prayer, 34
Preparation, 109
Pride, 47, 107
Protection, 9, 72, 97, 109
Proverbs, 22
Provision, 105, 120
Purpose, 126

R

Rain, 31
Reaping, 53
Reflection, 31
Refreshment, 73
Refuge, 8
Respect, 48, 52
Rest, 10, 47

S

Sabbath, 10
Sacrifice, 43, 113
Sadness, 85
Self-control, 76
Selfless, 78
Sharing, 105
Sin, 71
Sing, 102
Slaves, 54
Snow, 18
Stars, 26, 61
Stealing, 65
Storm, 23, 31

T

Talents, 100
Ten Commandments, 121
Thankful, 75, 81, 123
Treasure, 9, 66
Trust, 14, 65
Truthful, 126

W

Watchful, 21
Water, 45, 61
Widows, 28
Wisdom, 22, 87, 92
Wonders of the world, 94
Words, 47
Working, 70, 90

Z

Zacchaeus, 27

Inspired learning through great books.

Five in a Row is a complete,* well-rounded, literature-based curriculum that takes your child from pre-K through middle school.

Before Five in a Row

For ages 2-4

Before Five in a Row is a rich treasury of creative ideas that help you gently, consistently prepare your children for the lifelong adventure of learning. Now in a revised second edition, this bestselling volume is the foundation for inspired learning through great books and future studies with the entire Five in a Row curriculum.

More Before Five in a Row

For ages 3-5

More Before Five in a Row inspires your child's learning through extraordinary children's picture books while nurturing your relationship with them and making memories to last a lifetime! Designed for ages 3 through 5, this preschool and kindergarten curriculum is filled with lessons for you and your child to enjoy together and prepare your child for the lifelong adventure of learning.

Five in a Row

For ages 5-12

Five in a Row is an easy-to-follow, highly effective instructional guide for teaching Social Studies, Language Arts, Art, Applied Math and Science using outstanding children's literature as the basis for each unit study. Lessons are designed for children ages 5 through 12, and include discussion guide and questions, teacher answers, hands-on activities and suggestions for further study. Visit www.fiveinarow.com to view suggested age ranges for each volume.

Five in a Row Bible Supplements
(for Vols. 1-4 and 5-8)

The Five in a Row Bible Supplements, 2nd Editions, provide hundreds of lessons in character development with accompanying Bible references. Each story has numerous lessons to choose from, all in an easy-to-use format.

Full-Color, Laminated Story Disks

Available for *Before FIAR*, *More Before FIAR*, and *FIAR Volumes 1-5*.
Storybook Maps are also available for *Before FIAR* and *More Before FIAR*.

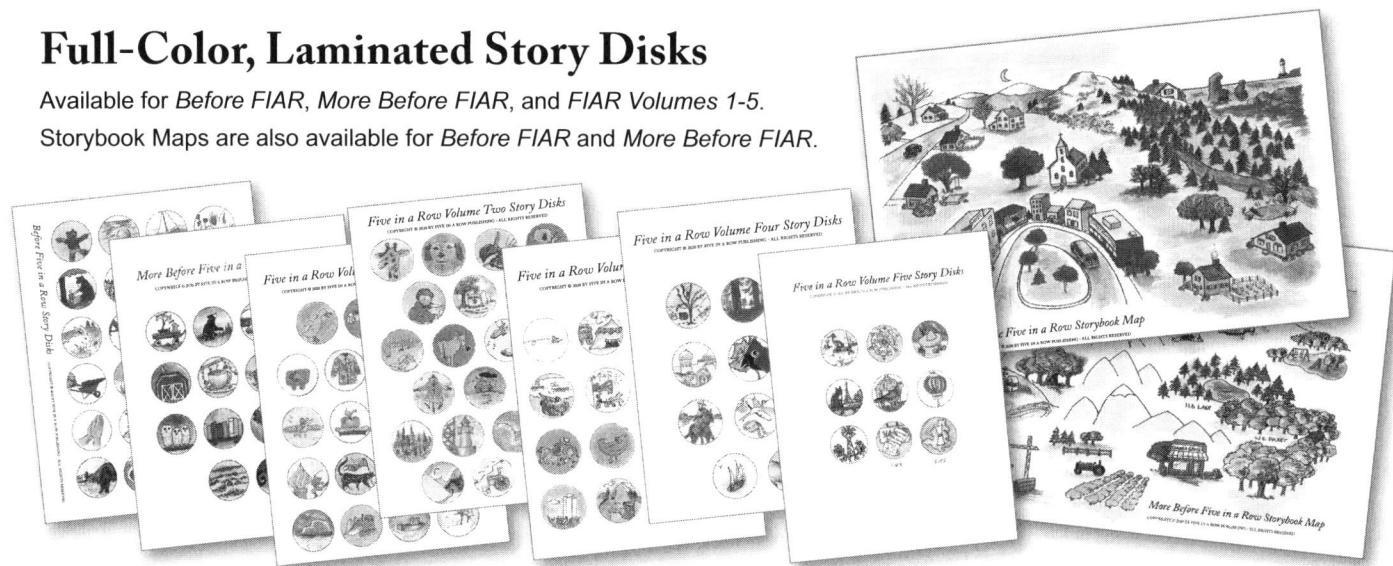

Digital Resources
Available from fiveinarow.com

FIAR Mini Units

Five in a Row Mini Units are digital unit studies based on children's picture books that include lessons for ages 2-12, designed to be used for one week.

FIAR Planner

The *Five in a Row Combined Family and Academic Planner* was created to give you access to school planning pages specific to the Five in a Row curriculum.

Notebook Builder

More than 120 pages of notebooking templates for all ages, appropriate for any topic or unit of study.

FIAR Nature Studies
(Spring, Summer, Fall, Winter)

FIAR Nature Studies encourage your entire family to enjoy and explore the outdoors in all four seasons. It is a true unit study approach to nature studies; suggestions introduce you and your child to poetry, music, and art that tie in to the season.

You will need to add math and phonics/reading instruction to **Five in a Row.*

www.fiveinarow.com

Made in the USA
Monee, IL
20 March 2023